David Linley   Design and Detail in the Home

David Linley

Design and Detail in the Home

Contributing Editor Janet Gleeson

Photographer Jan Baldwin

Little, Brown and Company

BOSTON · NEW YORK · LONDON

To my son Charles

I would particularly like to thank my wife Serena, Ruth Kennedy,
Tim Gosling, Jan Baldwin, Janet Gleeson, Ed Victor, Susannah Wass and
Juliet Gavin-Brown, without whom this book would not have been possible.

A Little, Brown Book

First published in 2000 by
Little, Brown and Company (UK).

Text by David Linley
© copyright 2000.

The moral right of the author has been
asserted.

A CIP catalogue for this book is
available from the British Library.

ISBN 0-316-85480-8

Designed by Andrew Barron &
Collis Clements Associates
Printed and bound in England by
Butler & Tanner

Little, Brown and Company (UK)
Brettenham House
Lancaster Place
London WC2E 7EN

Contents

Introduction

LOOKING AT THE PHOTOGRAPHS I HAVE SELECTED FOR THIS BOOK, what strikes me most forcefully is their variety. From the traditional long gallery of a country house to the minimalist London apartment, from the highly sophisticated to the simple, their diversity reflects my fondness for a multiplicity of styles.

The seeds of my disparate affections are probably rooted in my childhood. For as far back as I can remember I have been bombarded with old and new. My father was extremely fond of taking my sister and I on visits to interesting houses, selecting a broad variety of architectural styles for us to survey, from crumbling ancient monuments to ultra-modern houses. He often led us to believe that we had happened on the house in question quite by chance, and while he advanced confidently to knock on the door, my sister and I would cringe in embarrassment – and were duly amazed

(opposite) Detail of the much loved nineteenth-century rocking horse that I remember featuring prominently in my childhood. The horse's battered face has always had enormous appeal and now provides a rather unusual decorative element in my father's entrance hall. I have always enjoyed rooms in which the decorative objects play several roles, perhaps pleasing the eye, adding an element of surprise or telling a story that is personal to their owner, and this horse seems to fulfil all of these functions.

when the people who answered were so pleased to see him. As we walked through the rooms my father would tell us endless anecdotes about the history of the objects we were looking at, picking out unusual details for us to note. I well remember a visit to Rousham, when he showed me the furniture of William Kent and pointed out how extraordinary it was for his time. William Kent is a favourite of mine to this day.

Thanks to his clever and effortless manner we were taught to really look: at architecture, at rooms, at furniture and paintings, and also at the smaller details that help make an interior – the locks on a door, the legs on a piece of furniture, even the light-switches. Thus whether

we were confronted by an eighteenth-century cabinet or a tubular steel chair, we learned to appreciate the quality of its craftsmanship and the attention to detail that had gone into making it.

My father's appetite for wooden floors, stark white walls, metal shelving, egg chairs and the streamlined designs of Eero Saarinen, Alvar Aalto and Arne Jacobsen, was balanced by my mother's unerring taste for ballet, theatre and art exhibitions, and my early exposure to the richness of the interiors at various family homes. My mother also took us on memorable outings: to the Isle of Wight to see Osborne House, to picnic in the grounds of the Dutch House in Kew, to Eltham Lodge and the National Gallery. She is a brilliant judge of the low boredom threshold of children.

(opposite) My first experiments in interior decoration took place in my flat in Fulham. Two bicycles suspended on the wall in the hall-way were not as impractical as they sound, providing a surprisingly useful place to hang coats and umbrellas.

(right) The door in my father's kitchen has always been used to record the height of various members of the family.

I remember a visit to view the Leonardo cartoon at the National Gallery, and being told that if I liked the look of the other paintings hanging in the galleries I should come back to see them another time.

My mother also has distinctive taste. She has a particular penchant for rooms painted in strong colours – her garden room is raspberry pink, her drawing room a striking shade of turquoise – and for collecting shells and paintings by modern British artists such as Brian Organ, John Piper and Tony Fry.

My nascent interest in design was also nurtured by other members of the family. My grandmother is an incredible enthusiast for a vast spectrum of subjects. She sparked my fascination for mechanical furniture and secret compartments when she showed me a desk with a secret drawer in which she had found a hidden letter. When my paternal grandmother, Lady Rosse, came to visit she would come up to our bedrooms and ask to see our 'collections', even though at the time I think the only thing I actually collected was china animals. I also remember with a sense of fascination being taken to visit her brother, my great-uncle, the stage designer Oliver Messel, at his house in Pelham Crescent. We arrived at noon and I was astonished to see him appear at the door looking like Noël Coward (a friend of his) in his dressing gown. It was only later that I learned of his fondness for working through the night to complete his designs. Soon after I had started my business in Dorking, I sat down with my partner to make a Tuscan screen – the first of many we were to produce. We worked through till morning to complete it and I was told afterwards that this was just what my great-uncle had done.

When you are young, modernity, by its very nature, seems infinitely more interesting than convention. By the time I reached my early twenties and left Parnham House to begin designing furniture, my work showed little evidence of the traditional influences to which I'd been exposed. Aside, perhaps, from my enduring admiration

(opposite) A view of one end of the enormous living room in our apartment in Battersea. The piano in the far corner was not only useful when musically-inclined guests came to visit but also provided a wonderfully large area on which to display photographs. The walls were hung with an assortment of pictures we had collected over the years interspersed with some of our own works. A portrait of a rather unattractive ancestor was strategically placed behind the spiral staircase. The up lighter was designed by David Bristow from resin made to look like alabaster.

(left) A wonderful collection of treen made from various burr and fruitwoods, including snuff boxes in the form of shoes, clustered on a whatnot. Whether it is used for furniture or tiny objects such as these, I have always had a particular fondness for the warmth that wood invariably brings to a room.

for the traditions of fine craftsmanship, I was entirely bewitched by modern design. I established my business with the intention of following my inclination to produce modernist furniture, with the emphasis on good craftsmanship. However, little by little over the following years, and particularly after several visits to Venice during the 1980s, the past drew me back. Through books, houses and antique shops I began to rediscover a dictionary of ideas from which to draw and push forward. This reworking of traditional formats into something suited to modern-day living imbued me with a sense of new beginning. As I turned the pages of history I began to truly appreciate the furniture to which I'd been exposed for so many years. Now when I visit old houses I look with the eye of a cabinetmaker, and try to work out how old something is and how it was made.

My fascination for interiors is bound up with my interest in design. I remember painting a rather startling lightning strike across my bedroom ceiling at an early age, and even at school I had a tendency to move the dormitory furniture around. But it was only when I moved into my own flat in Fulham that I really had the time and scope to fall prey to the allure of decorating. For most of the ten years that I lived there I changed the colour of the walls in the drawing room twice a year, altering the chair covers to match with a variety of throws and shawls. I constructed new curtains with a staple gun – praying that no one would ever touch them because if they did they'd fall down on top of them – and when I was entertaining filled the room with flowers. I realised suddenly that a home of your own is more than just somewhere to hang your hat, it is also in a sense a stage set, somewhere to make an impression, to portray yourself in as many different ways as you choose.

For this reason I have always enjoyed interiors that surprise you. Alongside timeless classicism, I continue to admire the quirky, whether it's painting a wall black and hanging a bicycle on it for use as a coat rack, or

(opposite) A boldly furnished drawing room containing mainly modern pieces, including a side table by Linley and some dramatic pieces of modern art. The prominent fireplace and club fender balance the austerity of some of the furniture and bring a relaxed air to the room.

(right) An exact replica of the house in which it stands, this was one of the first house models made by Linley. Constructed from a multitude of woods, including sycamore, grey sycamore, ripple sycamore, vavona burr, English oak and rosewood, the model has a retractible roof that hides a small storage space, while parts of the façade are designed as drawers.

creating a picture from beads or carpentry tools or pencils, all of which feature on the following pages. Indeed, the novel and the conventional often work strikingly well side by side – one lightens and brightens, the other lends levity; together they create an interesting balance.

I learned the importance of meticulousness and attention to detail not only from my training as a cabinetmaker, but also, more painfully, from one or two memorable mistakes. In my flat at Burlington Lodge in Fulham I tried to recreate a faux mosaic effect on the bathroom floor using a layer of concrete. Unfortunately, the concrete was too thin; the floor looked wonderful but as soon as you stood on it the whole thing shattered. I was similarly foolhardy in my choice of burr oak for a front door. Burr

wood is usually cut from nodular growths at the root of a tree. With its intricate, tightly whorled figuring it looks wonderful, but it has very little inherent strength; an intruder's hand could easily have pushed straight through, though fortunately it never did.

As time passed and I moved into a larger apartment in Battersea, my fondness for mixing old with new became firmly entrenched, although I found my desire for change diminishing. This is the benefit of experience: as you learn what you like there seems little reason to alter it. If there's a secret to blending different styles, I think it's to do so with confidence. Buy what you like and you invariably find the right place for it somewhere, even if it's not where you expected and if the overall effect when placed against other objects surprises you.

The pleasure of a room comes not only from the colour of the walls and the objects in it, it is also dramatically altered by smell, temperature and lighting. It is amazing how easily ambience can alter by adjusting minor details. Of all the rooms I've been involved in designing I think my favourite is the drawing room in our flat in Battersea. Even though we no longer own it,

(opposite) Of the rooms that I have designed, the drawing room in our apartment in Battersea ranks among my favourites. The room measures about 100 feet long, but when we moved there consisted of three rooms. As well as knocking it into one we removed the ceilings to expose the beams and create a balancing sense of height.

(left) A self-portrait of Greg Powlesland, my ex-tutor at Parnham, is one of a wonderful assortment of interesting objects displayed in his study, alongside books, sculpture, old cameras, ships' models and interesting pebbles collected from the beach.

revisiting this room in the photographs reminds me of how adaptable the room could be. Lit entirely with candles it provided a wonderful space for parties; during the day sunlight streamed in and you could work happily there; it was also somewhere to watch TV or listen to music in comfort.

The diversity of styles within this book also highlights the various ways in which our homes reflect our lives and personalities: how we actually live as much as how we would like people to think we live. Some of the rooms featured on the following pages contain furnishings accumulated over many centuries, some are the sophisticated result of an interior designer's make over, some are intimate reflections of their occupants' lives and loves, while others epitomise the minimalist ideal of living pared back to its barest essentials, where almost nothing of the owner is revealed. All say something about their occupants and have something in them that I find fascinating and admirable, whether it's the carved legs on the furniture in a long gallery, the richness of the architectural detail in Bridgewater House, the sophistication of Bill Blass's elegant drawing room, or the stark purity of Stephen Bayley's living room, where to my mind the omissions are as interesting as the inclusions in more traditional room arrangements.

(opposite) Bill Blass's elegant New York apartment exemplifies the way in which contrasting styles can work successfully together. In his drawing room an elegant French Empire commode set beneath an eighteenth-century carved and gilded mirror provides a platform for what looks like a piece of contemporary sculpture but is in fact a Japanese wooden hook dating from the sixteenth century.

(right) A small low relief carving in white marble showing Cupid playing with a nymph; one of countless details that draw the eye in the ornate entrance hall of Bridgewater House.

Finding locations of such variety, setting them in their historical context and presenting them in a new and interesting way to highlight the details I particularly admire has proved an enjoyable challenge. I hope that by joining me on this journey through the home you will marvel as I do at the many distinctive styles and manners in which our homes may be shaped and so become sanctuaries of delight to all who enter there.

Finally, I would like to thank my family, friends and the other generous owners of the properties that feature on the following pages, who have so tolerantly allowed us to photograph their homes, and thus share the pleasure they evoke ✣

Keeley

THE ENTRANCE HALL BEGAN ITS EXISTENCE AS A ROOM WITH A
MULTITUDE OF FUNCTIONS. IN THE MEDIAEVAL HOUSE THE HALL WAS
THE ROOM IN WHICH GATHERINGS TOOK PLACE, BANQUETS WERE
EATEN, MUSICAL CONCERTS WERE PLAYED, OR VISITORS WAITED TO SEE
THE OWNER OF THE HOUSE. AS THE FIRST INTERIOR A VISITOR SAW,
THE ENTRANCE HALL WAS FAR MORE THAN A MERE PASSAGE TO ONE OF
THE MAIN ROOMS, AND AS SUCH WAS INVARIABLY DESIGNED TO LOOK
AS IMPRESSIVE AS POSSIBLE.

(opposite) The entrance hall at
Bridgewater House is dominated by its
dramatic ceiling. Designed by Sir
Charles Barry in the 1840s for Lord
Ellesmere, the hall was originally
intended to be an open courtyard but
later evolved into a magnificent room
covered with trellised glass panels. The
room is embellished with a wealth of
dazzling decoration such as these
plaster figures of Cupids and nymphs
surrounded by musical trophies.

Over time the function of the hall became less clear cut. By the eighteenth century it was often little more than a vestibule, a corridor from outside to in, a convenient spot in which to remove your hat and coat or leave your calling card.

Elsewhere, in grander houses the idea of creating an impact continued to flourish. Architects allowed their imaginations free rein, often looking to the ancient world for inspiration for their virtuoso creations. William Kent based his Marble Hall at Holkham, Norfolk, on a classical temple of justice, while at Kedleston in Derbyshire, Robert Adam created a striking hall based on a Roman atrium.

Today, whatever the size, scale or function of a hall, certain principles remain unchanged. A hall not only sets the tone for the house, it provides a pause from exterior to interior, somewhere to compose yourself before entering. Like William Kent and Robert Adam, I believe that entering a home should be exciting and surprising and I have always tried to include an element of the unexpected, unusual or something to amuse. You do not need a vast amount of space to treat an entrance imaginatively. My first, in my bachelor flat in Fulham, was a minute space filled with motorbike helmets, luggage and wine. I painted the walls black and hung two bicycles behind the door, which turned out to be both decorative and quite practical – they provided all sorts of interesting places to hang hats, scarves, coats and umbrellas.

The entry to Les Jolies Eaux, Mustique, was via a narrow path overflowing with hibiscus and bougainvillaea, which led you inside from a courtyard. In the entrance stood a metal side table, designed by my great-uncle, Oliver Messel; I had rescued it along with several other pieces of furniture from a skip. To add an element of surprise that was both personal and appropriate to the setting, my wife Serena and I painted a seascape which we hung above the table, arranging some locally made toy fishing boats directly in front of the canvas. Viewed from a certain angle the boats looked as if they really were sailing on the painted sea behind – and thus made the picture appear far more impressive than it really was.

In the Battersea apartment we confronted a rather awkwardly shaped space. A small entrance hall led to a long narrow corridor off which the main rooms opened. We treated the first space rather like an eighteenth-century print room, painting the walls duck-egg blue and covering them with prints, including a huge eighteenth-century map of Rome. The chiffonier is another of Oliver Messel's designs and is not nearly as old as it looks; the Chinese figures on top were a present from Hong Kong.

(opposite) A detail of the hallway of our Battersea apartment. As in all the rooms we mingled various styles and every object had some personal association. The Chinese figures were a gift from colleagues at work after a trip to Hong Kong and are supposed to bring good luck. The chiffonier came from my great-uncle Oliver Messel's house in Barbados; the chairs were given to me by my father.

They were in place for about a year before I realised that the ceremonial palanquin which is supposed to carry your spirit from this world to the next, was still in the box. Once I'd retrieved it I sought expert advice to make sure the figures were facing the most auspicious direction.

One of the things I like best about hallways is that they often provide an ideal space to show off visually striking but totally impractical furniture. I would put the chairs which stood in the hall – a gift from my father – into this category. Like most hall chairs they look good but you wouldn't want to sit on them for too long.

Our original intention was to use the long corridor leading from this area as a sculpture gallery. When this proved impractical we rationalised the space by dividing the walls into four and painting the sections yellow and terracotta alternately. Heavy cornicing and deep skirting boards helped pull the sections together and complemented the limestone floor, which we left bare. My favourite feature was the massive mahogany doors leading to the drawing room; each one measured twelve feet high. When I inherited these from a barn in Yorkshire they were in a state of dismal disrepair, having been left outside for twenty-five years. The veneer was lifting and had turned grey through exposure to the elements. Neither I nor the restorer realised quite how impressive they would turn out to be, but we were both delighted by the end result.

The other pieces of furniture in the corridor were all equally personal. The side table was a present from Hong Kong. I have owned the boat that sat on it since childhood. I vividly recall sailing it on the Round Pond in Kensington Gardens, where it invariably sank and had to be laboriously retrieved. The Portuguese chest underneath the table also belonged to me as a child and I remember it standing at the foot of my bed. The fan at the far end of the hall I bought in New York – it is over six feet tall and when switched on creates an extremely powerful breeze.

Including a sense of drama or surprise in an entrance hall helps build an atmosphere of anticipation about the rooms you are poised to enter. A popular way to achieve this sense of the unexpected is to display 'out of scale' objects. In the traditional entrance hall of the upstate New York house designed by Greg Jordan, a vast nineteenth-century painting of two children in an elaborate carved frame dominates the hallway. The picture is underlined by a low hall stool, based on an eighteenth-century style, made by Linley, and by two large pot plants.

(opposite) The corridor leading from the hallway provided another decorative challenge by virtue of its shape. It was long and narrow with very high ceilings. In order to draw the space in and make it feel less tunnel-like we divided the long walls into four and painted them alternate shades of terracotta and yellow. A heavy cornice made the ceiling seem less lofty, while a bare limestone floor added to the simplicity of the decorative scheme.

Hugh Henry has more idiosyncratic elements of surprise in the entrance hall of his London flat. The front door opens to reveal a vast unframed Russian painting of a hot air balloon ascent. Opposite stands a large and beautifully carved mahogany library table, above which hangs a mirror in a brightly coloured frame. A corridor leading from the entrance hall is sparsely furnished: a striped zebra skin rug propels the eye along towards the living room; a massive African drum provides a highly original departure from the usual side table.

One of the most dramatic yet subtle entrances I know is the hallway to Bill Blass's New York apartment. Here no detail has been overlooked in an attempt to create a strong initial impact. The dark and light criss-crossed floor is made from a combination of wood and stone. Lighting is concealed behind the cornice – a clever alternative to a central fitting or the ubiquitous down lighter. Angled walls provide the backdrop for a collection of architectural prints and drawings. The symmetrical structure of the architecture and the arrangement of the furniture lends a formality to the entrance and draws you into the living room beyond. A pair of columns with identical chairs set in front at an angle frame the doorway; behind, a pair of chiffoniers provide a platform for two equestrian bronzes, which again funnel you towards the door. A central pedestal on which a magnificent marble urn is displayed slightly obscures the light flooding in from the room beyond, thus softening the transition from outside to in.

Neutral shades unfailingly create an impression of timeless elegance and have always been popular for hallways as they provide an achromatic break between exterior and interior. Along with Bill Blass's ivory-painted entrance, four of the hallways featured here use this classic idea in very different ways. The most traditional, designed by Kelly Hoppen, is spanned by a wide three-centred arch which leads the eye towards the gentle curves of the staircase. Stone and mirrors are traditional features of hallways and here provide a dominant theme. The stone floor is echoed in a marble-topped table standing at the foot of the stairs, and a pair of stone-topped console tables over which hang a pair of large gilded mirrors.

When you enter Ann Boyd's entrance hall the first thing you notice, thanks to the generous use of scented candles, is a delicious smell. Ann has given the conventional neutral colour scheme and furniture arrangement a clever personal twist. Space here is restricted, thus instead of the traditional arrangement of a pair of mirrors over side

(opposite) The entrance to Ann Boyd's London apartment shows how easily elegance combines with unusual quirky details. The space is minimal, yet a clever use of neutral shades, subtle lighting and touches of colour provides plenty of visual interest. Up lighters concealed behind a clutch of blue and white vases throw dramatic shadows over a montage of African mother-of-pearl beads taken from a necklace.

tables, one entire wall is mirrored, making the area seem twice as large and much lighter. Under the side table a pair of gilt-framed mirrors are propped against the skirting board. The side table provides a stage for a collection of blue and white porcelain jars. These have been carefully arranged in a cluster to hide up lighters illuminating an ingeniously displayed collection of African beads in a large wooden frame.

In my father's London home – an early nineteenth-century end-of-terrace house – neutral shades are intertwined with vivid splashes of colour. You enter through glossy black-painted double doors to a hallway complete with stone floor, staircase and marbled columns. Within this typical Regency interior the balustrade is painted a brilliant shade of lapis-lazuli blue, while a lamp at the foot of the stairs echoes the same shade. A few unusual objects add further visual interest: the fans on the wall and the drum table in front of them seem to echo the curving sweep of the staircase; the nineteenth-century rocking horse is a family treasure that he inherited from his grandfather; the cage contains a singing automaton bird.

Small architectural details, such as the variety of interesting doorknobs, also provide notes of individuality that are entirely characteristic of my father. Those on the front door resemble eagles' claws, while others are cast as roses. As in most rooms my father has decorated, there is an element of the unpredictable; not all is quite as it seems. The fanlight over the front door looks both delicate and in keeping with the Regency building, but I remember him making it from plastic mouldings dipped into hot water so they would bend, basing the design on Georgian fanlights he had admired in Dublin.

The entrance hall to the furniture designer Sir Ambrose Heal's house also manages to combine the traditional with highly personal touches. A traditional oak dresser and mahogany is used with a 1920's painted wood chair. Largely a result of the texture of bare wood on the doors, floors and beams, with their naive stencilling, what strikes you most about this entrance is the warmth of its atmosphere.

Scale of a completely different order is evoked by the incredible hallway of a family house in Worcestershire. Construction was recorded on the site from the twelfth century, and parts of the existing house can be traced back to Tudor times, although most of what exists today dates from the nineteenth century when the building was extensively altered. This grand, spacious hallway began life as three rooms, and was knocked into one, evidently with a view to impressing visitors. Now it comfortably

(opposite) The hallway of my father's London home always delights me for the beguiling way in which architecture, decoration and furniture have been combined to such simple yet dramatic effect. The wrought iron balustrade is painted a brilliant shade of blue which is echoed in the lamp below. The serpentine line of the staircase and its balustrade provides a niche for a circular drum table, and curving lines are mirrored in the fans mounted on the wall behind.

holds fifteen or twenty people and is packed with a cacophony of colour, pattern and texture – all in all about as far from neutral shades and classical restraint as it is possible to imagine. Three huge glass domes throw pools of light into a vast two-storey galleried hall. The walls – dark oak panelled below, white above – are hung with an array of family portraits and 'The Quarries of Syracuse', a famous painting by Edward Lear.

To my mind, the most remarkable feature of this room is the crystal balustrade which is believed to be unique. In such a vast hallway the furniture needs to be similarly generously proportioned. The great Italian marble fireplace forms a central point around which large sofas and stools are arranged. Scattered about the room, all manner of family memorabilia accumulated over the centuries provides plenty to look at and admire, and you cannot help wondering at the story behind the seventeenth-century Augsburg apothecary's cabinet, or the grand pair of lanterns bought by a previous owner and now standing on either side of the chimney piece.

Finally – although it is hard to top the last hall – to what seems to me to be the most remarkable entrance to any private house in London. The hallway of Bridgewater House, St James's, never fails to astonish me for its unbridled opulence. The house was built in 1854 by Sir Charles Barry (the architect of the Palace of Westminster) in a grand Italianate style, and much of the original interior survives (despite suffering severe bomb damage during the war), including this overwhelming galleried entrance hall. Unlike so many gloomy Victorian entrances, Barry has cleverly maximised natural daylight. Originally intended as an open court, Barry decided to cover the area with a domed atrium surrounded by smaller lights of pyramid-shaped glass that flood the vast space below with natural light. On a bright day so much light streams through that the lamps look as though they're switched on even when they're not.

In the tradition of grand hallways through the ages, the space serves not just as an entrance but also somewhere in which concerts and receptions are held; appropriately enough, the gallery ceiling is peppered with allusions to Greek mythology, with particular reference to musical themes. As you gaze upward there is a wealth of detail to attract the eye, from the Italian frescoes to marble low-relief carvings of putti, while even the specially woven Axminster carpet reflects the rich hues of the wall decorations. As a visitor presented with such a staggering abundance of detail, the only drawback is tearing yourself away to enter the rest of the house �֍

(opposite) This staircase hall is dramatic in its scale yet still manages to seem friendly in the country house atmosphere it conveys. An adaptable space that also serves as a living area, it contains a wealth of family treasures including a vast assortment of family portraits assembled over the years. The three large glass domes providing pools of light were installed by a nineteenth-century owner who chose the motto emblazoned on the cornice beneath them: 'Shadows fly: life like a dome of many coloured glass stains the white radiance of eternity until death tramples it to fragments . . .'

(above) Small details provide a balance to the overall drama of the hall. Here a box is delightfully inlaid with a geometric pattern of ivory.

(above right) The galleried landing in the staircase hall with its crystal balustrades is believed to be the only one of its kind. The staircase was installed in the nineteenth century when the hall was created from three smaller rooms.

(opposite) A carving of Cupid on an ebony press cupboard reveals the extraordinary skill of seventeenth-century craftsmen. The dramatic colour and close texture of ebony made it popular for cabinetmaking, although it was one of the hardest woods to carve.

(opposite) The spacious hallway of this London house designed by Kelly Hoppen combines elegant restraint with a few carefully chosen touches of drama, such as the pair of marble-topped side tables with their griffin bases, an extravagant vase of flowers, and the large gilded mirrors.

(below) The entrance of Sir Ambrose Heal's country house is dominated by a heavy oak-beamed ceiling dating from the sixteenth century. The stencilling lightens the effect and was added in the 1920s when the house was extensively restored by Sir Ambrose Heal. Much of the furniture was designed by him, and reflects his admiration for traditional craftsmanship.

(far left) The painted decoration of the entrance to Bridgewater House was commissioned by Lord Ellesmere from the German artist Jakob Götzenberger, who also designed the plaster figures decorating the ceiling.

(left) Saucer domes designed by Sir Charles Barry are framed by elaborate gilded plaster work. Although this was not part of Barry's original scheme, it adds significantly to the overall opulent effect.

(opposite) Mouldings on the upper storey of Bridgewater House reflect the classical Italianate theme with characteristic Corinthian pilasters, acanthus scrolls and flower heads.

(opposite) On sunny days so much light comes through the glass domes at Bridgewater House that the lamps beneath look as if they are switched on. The Italianate painted decoration includes delicate grotesques, floral designs and armorials by Jakob Götzenberger, a nineteenth-century German artist renowned for his murals. (right) The dazzling effect of marble, scagliola, painted decoration, gilding and plaster work decorations combined in such abundance strikes visitors as soon as they enter the palatial entrance hall. The colourful carpet was specially designed to reflect the powerful architecture of the room as part of recent renovations.

(left) The family rocking horse dates from the late nineteenth century and has been played with by generations of children. My father inherited it from his grandfather and it now acts as an attractive and unusual adornment in his hallway.

(below left) My father's meticulous eye for detail is reflected in his choice of carefully collected door knobs. The front door features a brass eagle's claw holding a ball, while one of the inside doors is fitted with this attractive rosebud handle.

(opposite) View from the hallway to the front door. The fan light is based on eighteenth-century door lights that my father had seen in Dublin and was made by him from plastic mouldings bent in hot water and painted to look like lead.

(left) The timeless elegance of interior designer Hugh Henry's hallway relies on a clever combination of antique and modern furniture and rigorously controlled use of colour and pattern. Here a pair of suede upholstered chairs flank a mahogany library table, while a large mirror in a brightly coloured frame provides a touch of colour.

(right) In the corridor leading off the hallway Hugh Henry has banished bright colours in favour of a monochrome scheme, and used a few strong objects to soften the long, narrow space. A huge African drum makes a break in a long wall; the strong patterns on a zebra skin rug lead your eye towards the living room beyond.

(opposite left) The walls of designer Bill Blass's apartment are used as a display area for an extensive collection of architectural drawings, watercolours and prints. The restricted use of colour ensures the overall feel is not of clutter but of calm serenity. Architecture is centred around the focal point of the door to the living room: the criss-cross black and white stone floor centres on the doorway, while the walls are also angled towards the door with prints, furniture and sculpture arranged symmetrically on either side. A pair of heavy fluted white columns form a frame, while a pedestal with a vast onyx urn from Pavlosk Palace in Russia acts as a partial barrier, softening the light streaming in from the living room beyond.

(above and left) The hallway of this house in upstate New York designed by Greg Jordan shows how 'out of scale' objects can be used in hallways to striking effect. Here, a large painting of two children is framed by a long hall stool made by Linley, and a towering pair of potted plants.

THE FORMAL LIVING ROOM BEGAN AS THE MEDIAEVAL GREAT CHAMBER —
A PUBLIC ROOM USED FOR FORMAL GATHERINGS AND FEASTS. THE
GREAT CHAMBER WAS TYPICALLY HIGH-CEILINGED, WITH WALLS HUNG
WITH TAPESTRIES OR LARGE PICTURES AND SEAT FURNITURE
ARRANGED AROUND THE EDGE.

(opposite) One of the classical figures that frame a mid-eighteenth-century marble chimney piece in the centre of the Long Gallery. The chimney piece is believed to have been carved by Mr Scheemaker, a Huguenot craftsman. Many of the classical mouldings it features are echoed elsewhere in the room. The elaborately carved and gilded moulding behind also forms the dado and includes c-scrolls, key motif and egg and dart moulding.

The informal living room started out as a 'withdrawing room'. In contrast to the great chamber, this was a private space often adjoining a bedroom, to which a family might retreat in search of privacy. As comfort became increasingly important, withdrawing rooms were made more cozy and intimate with low ceilings and expensive furnishings, such as elaborately carved tables, coffers and cupboards, and tapestry, velvet or silk hangings.

During the eighteenth century the distinction between the formal and private remained clear. Modest homes might have a front parlour used only on special occasions, while in grand houses the great chamber evolved into the saloon or gallery, and the less formal drawing room was used for leisure pursuits such as card playing or musical recitals.

The combination of separate drawing room and informal living room remains popular in countless Victorian and Edwardian (and more recent) houses, but in modern times the distinction between formal and private living rooms has become increasingly blurred, resulting in a single multi-purpose room. Nowadays, a living room may be somewhere family treasures are displayed, parties are held, books are read, the television is watched – everyone has an idea of how their living room should be. But whatever their use, they invariably provide an insight into the way people live – and a glimpse of the way they would like to be perceived. My own feeling is that when space is at a premium, as it often is, it seems a shame not to use it to its full potential. Perhaps the ideal solution is to have a living room in which family and friends can spend time together in comfort, and a study to retreat to when you want to be alone.

One of the most dramatic differences between an eighteenth- and a twentieth-century living room is in the seating. While we now take a squashy sofa and armchairs almost for granted whatever the size and style of the living room, two hundred years ago these did not feature as sprung upholstery was not available until the nineteenth century. Before this time seating tended to be arranged around the sides of the room, to be pulled into the centre when necessary. In the eighteenth century chair-making became a highly specialised occupation. An astonishing variety of shapes and forms of chair were made; most were not designed to sink into or loll about in, but to maintain the dignity of their occupant, although day beds and chaise longues were popular for more relaxed moments. Even though people were forced to sit reasonably straight-backed on most seats, comfort was important. As Sheraton wrote in his cabinet

(opposite) The Long Gallery epitomises a traditionally furnished formal living area in which furniture and paintings assembled over the centuries are shown off to perfection. Apart from the odd dim electric light, scarcely anything has changed here for the last two hundred years, and everywhere you look there is a wealth of detail that highlights the skills of traditional craftsmanship.

dictionary: 'Chair-making is a branch generally confined to itself, as those who professedly work at it seldom engage to make cabinet furniture . . . The two branches seem evidently to require different talents in workmen, in order to become proficient. In the chair branch it requires a particular turn in the handling of shapes, to make them agreeable and easy'.

One of my favourite formal living rooms is a highly traditional Long Gallery in a house in the west of England. The room provides an intriguing view of how a grand living room in a large country house was once furnished. There are almost no twentieth-century intrusions apart from the odd (dim) electric light. The walls are covered with green damask silk, hung with fine family portraits and other paintings,

and the furniture is made by some of the leading eighteenth-century cabinetmakers of the day. But perhaps because everything has remained unchanged for so long, when you enter the room you feel a sense of harmony rather than ostentation.

Among the most striking pieces in the room are the suite of day beds and stools, upholstered in green damask

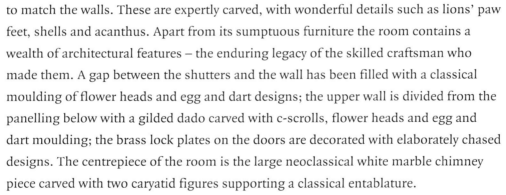

(above) The skill and imagination of eighteenth-century carvers is reflected in the amazing variety of feet adorning the furniture: (from left to right) gilded mahogany lions'-paw feet on a day bed; eagles'-claw feet on a chair; claw feet on the lacquer stand of a Chinese export games cabinet.

to match the walls. These are expertly carved, with wonderful details such as lions' paw feet, shells and acanthus. Apart from its sumptuous furniture the room contains a wealth of architectural features – the enduring legacy of the skilled craftsman who made them. A gap between the shutters and the wall has been filled with a classical moulding of flower heads and egg and dart designs; the upper wall is divided from the panelling below with a gilded dado carved with c-scrolls, flower heads and egg and dart moulding; the brass lock plates on the doors are decorated with elaborately chased designs. The centrepiece of the room is the large neoclassical white marble chimney piece carved with two caryatid figures supporting a classical entablature.

No matter what its scale or style, creating a relaxing, comfortable and intimate atmosphere is perhaps more important in a living room than in any other room in the house. When I think of my favourite living rooms, it is invariably the happy times spent in them that I remember rather than the objects they contain, and this must be a testimony, in part at least, to the mood created by the room. Colour, lighting, furniture, flooring, decorative items, even flowers and plants; all play a part in creating this welcoming feel.

(above) The lock plate on the door
illustrates the sophistication of
metalwork in the eighteenth century.
Featuring family armorials and
winged cherub heads, the plate has all
the refinement of a piece of silverware.

In large rooms such as the Long Gallery, one way to create a sense of intimacy is to divide the room by the arrangement of the furniture. This was a lesson I learned when tackling the living room of my apartment in a converted school house in Battersea. The living room had started life as a series of rooms, which I made into one, opening it up to the roof to reveal the rafters and thus creating a vast and challenging living room which measured one hundred feet long. I have always enjoyed moving furniture around to try out different effects, but as in any interior the eventual arrangement of the room was largely determined by what we had available. Because it was such a large area I knew it was important to include some large pieces to pull the room together. The fireplace – made from an old door frame in one afternoon with the help of a carpenter – created the central point of the living area, and we installed double doors to give a sense of balance on either side.

Temperature is of course vital in creating a warm atmosphere. A fireplace, whether real or a gas imitation, creates a visual focal point as well as warmth towards which people always gravitate. For this reason I have always been fond of club fenders, which have the added bonus of allowing people to perch on them and warm themselves in comfort while chatting.

Floors are another important and often neglected detail that can add greatly to the atmosphere of a room. In the Battersea apartment we resisted the temptation to sand down the roughened old boards, and instead made something of a feature of all the signs of wear and tear, by simply varnishing the floor dark brown and using two large rugs to divide the dining end from the sitting area. The floor thus retained its original character and added an extra and rather homely dimension to the room.

The living room is one of the most satisfying places in a house in which to display things, because you can be sure people have time to sit and enjoy them. By using oddly contrasting objects and furniture – an old tool chest instead of a side table, or a couple of varnished logs for fireside seats – I like to tease people and give them plenty to keep them interested. In large rooms furniture can be used to divide a wall space or lead the eye to a group of pictures or objects. Clustering things together informally while keeping a natural balance, perhaps using a picture rail and dado as a framework, can make quite ordinary objects look more important and create a more striking effect than dotting things sparsely around the walls. Flowers, whether large or small, provide a wonderful lift to every room, especially the living room, and when I am entertaining I

(opposite) View of the drawing room of our apartment in Battersea, showing how the furniture was arranged to divide the vast space into clearly defined areas. The focal point of the central seating area was the fireplace. Beyond it stood the vast dining table originally made for my father-in-law's house, Baynton, and four huge bookcases salvaged from a cellar and restored.

always try to buy flowers a day or two early so they have opened and scented the room by the time the guests arrive.

In any living room, no matter how large or small, using side lights on tables, old-fashioned picture lights positioned on the wall, the often derided standard lamps (which I personally like), and candles for special occasions, is far more flattering, both to the room and the people in it, than overhead lights. Even light switches can add to the harmony of a decorative scheme. I always try to conceal switches in a dado rail or on a wall return. In the apartment in Battersea I used squares of glass backed with wallpaper rather than conventional switches which look intrusive.

The epitome of a formal drawing room, and the smartest living room I know in New York, is that belonging to the designer Bill Blass. The architecture of the room is carefully thought out. Panelling and an elaborate cornice soften the walls and contrast richly with a dark hard-wood floor. Notice how the bevelled edges of the boards add depth to the floor and reflect the light. The feeling of formality is emphasised by the symmetrical arrangement of the furniture – a carefully chosen melange of antique and modern. I can't imagine lounging on the elegant Empire-style chaise longues that frame the fireplace; they are the type of furniture that demands a certain decorum, but they certainly contribute to the sophistication of the room.

Dramatic and dynamic in its use of black, white and gold is the living room of a New York apartment belonging to a Swedish financier, designed by Anouska Hempel, Linley and Charles Allen. Before the room was furnished the architecture of the entire apartment was painstakingly altered so that the doors lined up to provide an impressive enfilade reminiscent of grand eighteenth-century apartments. Once again, the predominantly symmetrical arrangement of the furniture and the choice of Empire style lend a sense of formality. The severity of the scheme is softened by the lighting. Moulded glass ceiling lights echo the enfilade and lead the eye to the next room, while a side lamp by Tiffany provides a warm glow. The carpet has been hand painted to reflect the colour scheme. A visual barrier between this room and the hallway beyond is created by a pair of tall cabinets with two chairs placed in front.

A suite of rooms leading into each other is also to be found in Princess Salimah Aga Khan's London home. Here, however, there is a notable change in mood and colour as you move from one room to the next. The red-gold tones of the upholstery in the first drawing room have a sumptuous warmth that suggests a room tailored to

(opposite) The sumptuous Empire-style black and gold drawing room of a New York apartment designed for a Swedish financier. A sense of space is created by the formal enfilade arrangement of the rooms, with wide doorways and glass ceiling lights drawing the eye from one room to the next. Black cornices and skirtings bring strong definition to each room.

evening use. The bold use of gold brings a touch of brilliance to the scheme. Mouldings on the door frames and cornice are highlighted in gilding, and on either side of the door a superb pair of English gilt-wood Rococo mirrors, designed by Thomas Johnson in the mid-eighteenth century, continue the golden theme. Double doors lead you through to a second drawing room. As you enter this sunny room with its windows overlooking Hyde Park, the first thing you notice is the chimney-piece wall decked with a vast collection of seventeenth-century botanical prints by Dutch artist Hendrick Adrina Van Rheade tot Draakestein. This wonderful display makes you feel you are in a garden, and the pale green and yellow colour scheme harmonises perfectly with this airy outdoor feel. I love the way the huge mirror over the green chimney piece reflects the enfilade of doorways behind, and the way the ranks of tulips on the mantelpiece continue the botanical theme.

In the flat of well-known interior designer Alidad, two interconnecting rooms have been similarly linked together and decorated to suit different moods and times of the day. In the morning you can sit in the bright, sunny yellow room with the sun streaming through the windows. In the evening, the rich red painted walls and ceiling, blazing fire and candle light create a snug, intimate ambience at the opposite end of the room. This coziness is partly created by the comfortable clutter. Interesting textiles are softly draped over a door and a fender seat, whilst the bookshelves have been cleverly used both as storage space for books and to display objects.

In the drawing room of a country house in upstate New York designed by Greg Jordan, colour and light contribute to the feeling of warmth that is your first impression of the room. This is a sumptuous room which cleverly manages not to seem overpowering – largely a result, I think, of the attractive collections of objects and family photographs. The owner's fondness for flowers is reflected in the lovely arrangement on the table, which seems to draw together the warm pinks and greens of the furnishings, as well as the tapestry cushions and attractive needlepoint rug.

Marrying a feeling of space with a sense of coziness is one of the greatest challenges in designing a living room. In John and Sarah Standing's living room the great luxury of plenty of natural light, high ceilings and the open arch leading to the white kitchen-dining room beyond, creates the first impression of airiness. This is a room in which small detail has created a balance between informal and formal: warm stippled pink walls and chintz upholstery are balanced by a classical stencilled frieze; a

(opposite) The drawing room of John and Sarah Standing's London home has an imposing air with its generously high ceilings, yet it has been carefully tailored for relaxed family living. Soft pink ragged walls create a warm backdrop for a collection of paintings and match the cheerful chintz upholstery. An eclectic mix of family photographs, objets d'art and books give the room a comfortable atmosphere, and the wide archway leading into the kitchen ensures that even when you are cooking you never feel cut off from the conversation.

large traditional wooden sofa table is contrasted with a modern mirror-topped table; the assorted photographs, books, plants and objects imbue the room with the personality of its owners.

A collection of art, books and artefacts assembled over a lifetime in the London apartment of a retired diplomat creates a living room with an enviable chic about it. I like the way the long table, draped so vividly with a blue cloth, is arranged with an assortment of books, ceramics, glass and other objects. There is a feeling here that nothing is static, that you are being invited to pick things up and look at them. Behind the table is a winning arrangement of prints, watercolours and oils. The wall on the left is cleverly mirrored which adds to the feeling of space and light.

In Ann Boyd's drawing room a softly muted colour scheme conveys an atmosphere of roominess within a far more restricted space. Everything has been carefully coordinated to tally with the subtle shades of the room: elegant ceramics in celadon blue and cream stand on a low table; the upholstery is in muted tones of blue and grey; external window boxes filled with lavender echo a pair of purple upholstered window seats placed inside; flowers in small vases dotted about the room bring softness as well as a delicious scent. And, as a final touch, even the dog matches the scheme!

Restrained colours are used to create a far more masculine effect in Hugh Henry's sitting room. As in the previous example, the use of neutral colours brings a sense of calm – even though the flat is in central London with traffic rattling the windows. This restful ambience is partly achieved by arranging furniture and paintings symmetrically, but not fiercely so, to give a sense of balance. Restricting colour helps the eye to focus on the multiple textures within the room: the rough linen weave of the sofa contrasts with the satin cushions; the richly polished marquetry commode is used to display a specimen of coral and a white marble low relief carving; on the table next to the sofa a smooth black polished stone carving is set against a mineral specimen, the spines of leather bound books and the cold surfaces of the marble and steel fireplace.

Even more austere in its absence of colour and ornament is the drawing room of the style guru Stephen Bayley. There are no pictures on the walls, no carpets, none of the usual paraphernalia you expect in a family house. Visual interest is provided by the shadows cast from the glasses perched on a strange slit in the wall that divides the drawing room from the entrance hall. Rather like an empty stage, this is a room in which people rather than furniture must provide the colour and ambience ❖

(opposite) Neutral shades, soft blues, lavenders and celadon greens characterise the drawing room of designer Ann Boyd's home. An interesting collection of ceramic bowls on a low table and a large pitcher placed underneath an abstract painting in similar muted shades, continues the subtle theme. Despite its studied restraint the room contains some witty touches. I like the way the lavender window seats match the lavender growing in the window boxes outside.

(left) A summery morning room in which neutral walls provide a backdrop for a wonderful collection of hand-coloured seventeenth-century Dutch botanical prints. The floral theme is continued in the five vases of tulips arranged on the green marble chimney piece. A large looking glass and chandelier add richness and light. The morning room is linked by double doors to the drawing room (above). This is decorated in a richer palette of crimson and gold that makes it an ideal room for the evening. The pair of mirrors on either side of the doorway were designed by the leading eighteenth-century cabinetmaker Thomas Johnson and featured in his book of designs published in 1758.

(below) Side tables in the drawing room of an upstate New York house designed by Greg Jordan display an interesting collection of antique snuff boxes, scent bottles and paperweights.

(right) A table placed against the wall in the drawing room provides a useful surface on which to display a vast array of books and art objects. There is an appealing informality to this arrangement which makes you feel as if you are being invited to pick things up and admire them.

(left) In Stephen Bayley's drawing room all superfluous decoration and colour has been banished in favour of a pared down, uncluttered look. The upholstery is plain white, and there are no pictures, rugs or curtains. A section of the wall between the living room and hallway has been removed to form a glazed display space for a collection of antique glasses.

(right) Another corner of the drawing room in our Battersea apartment. When I lived in my flat in Fulham I would often hand a chisel to friends who visited and ask them to carve their names into the surface of my dining table. By the time I moved, the table had too many happy associations to ignore. Even though I no longer needed it for its original purpose I decided to use it as an unusual decoration on the wall, where guests could continue the tradition. In front are two varnished logs which served as rather precarious fireside seats, two corrugated paper lamps and a collection of Chinese blue and white plates.

(right) Drawing room belonging to an art connoisseur, arranged as a showcase for a fascinating collection of furniture and paintings. The room is traditionally organised around a plain white marble chimney piece on which stand bronze candelabra, an elegant pair of porcelain vases and a nineteenth-century ormolu French clock. Warm apricot walls and splashes of vivid crimson counter the formal way in which the furniture and paintings are positioned and make the room feel both elegant and cozy. (left) In one corner an enviable collection of treen boxes, some featuring intricate marquetry decoration, is clustered on a whatnot.

(opposite) Muted black and white tones and natural textures are a key note in Bill Blass's elegant drawing room. The plainness of the decoration is ideally suited to the impressive collection of classical sculptures displayed in the room, and much of the furniture continues the classical theme. The low table in the foreground is based on a Roman design copied by C. H. Tatham in the nineteenth century; the elegant chaise longue is also reminiscent of Roman sofas and day beds; while (below) a circular Empire-style table adorned with an anthemion flower frieze and classical caryatid supports is used to display a circular tortoiseshell snuffbox.

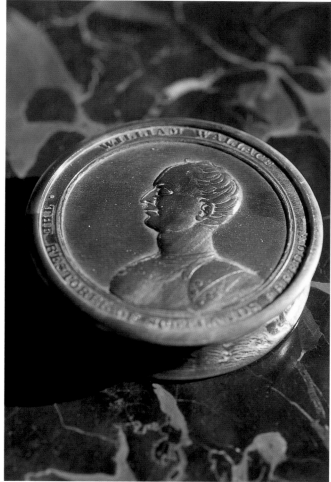

(left and below) Hugh Henry's drawing room epitomises understated refinement, but its eclectic mix of furniture and decorative objects such as African art and geological specimens ensures it is far from conventional. The room is decorated in shades of white, with the brightest colour provided by splashes of crimson in the carpet. The focal point of the room is the grey marble fireplace above which hangs a nineteenth-century French mirror with a delicate serpentine frame. On the mantelpiece in front are three African masks made from painted wood. The sofa continues the subtle colours of the walls and is upholstered in Linley linen. To the right is an elegant nineteenth-century Italian commode richly veneered in a parquetry design.

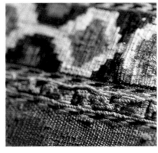

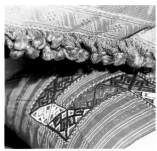

(both pages) The sumptuous multi-layered effect of the drawing room in Alidad's flat is created by opulent paintwork and a multitude of textiles. The proliferation of pattern brings a warm and friendly feel to the room. Even the door is brought into the decorative scheme: it has been painted to match the walls and also provides a useful backdrop on which to display a fragment of antique tapestry. A fat red cord thrown around the handle in an extravagant swag provides further richness. Elsewhere, a variety of European and Middle Eastern embroidered and woven textiles are draped over furniture and every surface is crammed with a large variety of decorative objects, including a striking bronze bust of the dancer Nijinsky by Una Trubridge.

(opposite) Filled with morning sunlight and with walls painted a vivid shade of yellow, the opposite end of Alidad's drawing room is ideally suited to daytime living. The yellow theme reverberates in a yellow sofa and a pair of yellow lamps on the chimney piece, while curtains of olive green are reflected in a stencilled door frame. Touches of crimson in the patterned cushions and Persian rug provide a link between this end of the room and its counterpart. The jewel-like ambience of the room is emphasised by the profusion of treasures displayed here (see below), including a plaster bust of the Roman emperor Augustus and a tiara bought from a junk shop and believed to have been made originally to adorn a statue of the Virgin Mary.

Chapter 3   Dining

SIDEBOARDS, DINING TABLES, CHAIRS, URNS, WINE COOLERS,
CELLARETS AND PLATE WARMERS OF ENORMOUS VARIETY AND
ELEGANCE FILL THE PAGES OF DESIGN BOOKS BY EIGHTEENTH-
CENTURY CABINETMAKERS SUCH AS CHIPPENDALE, HEPPLEWHITE AND
SHERATON. BY THE LATE EIGHTEENTH CENTURY, THE DINING ROOM,
FOR WHICH ALL THESE ITEMS WERE MADE, HAD REPLACED PARLOURS
AND GREAT HALLS IN MOST LARGE HOUSES AS AN ESSENTIAL PART OF
THE DOMESTIC LAYOUT, ONE OF THE MOST IMPORTANT AND IMPOSING
OF RECEPTION ROOMS.

(opposite) The walls of Alidad's dining
room are hung with leather painted
with a bold design of intertwining
flowers and fruits. Throughout the
centuries leather was a traditional wall
covering for dining rooms since it was
believed not to retain lingering food
smells. A large mirror positioned over
the fireplace amplifies the soft light of
candles mounted in large church
candlesticks and crystal salts. An alium
in a pot seems to reflect the simple
plant forms of the wall covering.

Apart from providing somewhere to eat and drink in grand style, the dining room offered the home owner the opportunity to create a splendid setting in which to show off his eye-catching collection of silver, glass and porcelain. Because the dining room was used on formal occasions, and often at night, it was, by its very nature, suited to the most dramatic of decor.

Nevertheless, not all were entirely wholesome or elegant. One foreign visitor to London in 1710 was utterly disgusted by what he saw of the dining hall at Middle Temple: 'The table had just been laid, and on it were wooden platters and green earthenware pots, into which the bones are cast; there were no napkins and the table-cloth looked as if a sow had just had a litter on it. We had no desire to dine there, and we hastened to look at the Library.' Even in the late eighteenth century, meals were far from refined. Sophie Von Roche, a visitor to London in 1786, explained what she believed to be the reason for the gargantuan scale of some of the serving dishes: '... because a quarter of a calf, half a lamb and monstrous pieces of other meats are dished up, and everyone receives almost an entire fish ...'

Unlike these disgruntled observers, I always think of dining rooms, whether modern or traditional, sumptuous or simple, as generally cheerful places, and despite the modern trend to do away with them in favour of a larger kitchen that is used every day, I still harbour a lingering fondness for them. Some of my earliest childhood memories are of dining rooms filled with the warm smell of red wine and Gauloises, of talking, laughter and discussions (most of which I didn't understand) going on around the table. I also remember being deeply impressed by the way in which the table was laid, flowers arranged and ornaments set out, and this has remained a lasting concern. I still enjoy interesting and unusual table arrangements, whether they are as simple as a bunch of flowers arranged in a bread bin or a table covered with night-lights, or as extravagant as a vast display of flowers several feet high.

The most important single object in any dining room is the table. At Burlington Lodge I had my first proper opportunity to decorate a dining room. I designed a gothic-style table made from oak, with a heavy glass top which I thought would be practical to keep clean. In fact, though it was often quite amusing to watch people becoming friendly under the table – for some reason they never realised they could be seen – I eventually changed the top because it always felt uncomfortably cold to the touch.

The second table top was made from some beautiful burr oak planks I discovered

(opposite) Lighting is the key to the theatrical ambience of Alidad's dining room. The room is lit only by candles, and heavy shutters exclude all daylight. The richness of the wall covering is complemented by an equally elaborately painted ceiling and the dark marble chimney piece.

about to be thrown away in a timber yard. These were simply joined together, sanded and polished, although the surface was left fairly rough and uneven. Whenever anyone came to dinner I handed them a chisel and invited them to carve their initials in the top. Some people were amazingly imaginative – a carver 'wrote' in a continuous line without once removing the chisel. I became so fond of the top that when I moved to Battersea I decided to keep the tradition going by screwing the table top to the wall and continuing to invite people to carve their initials on it. On entering the dining room and seeing a huge piece of wood fixed to the wall, one visitor asked what it was. I told them it was a table, to which they replied, 'Isn't it rather tricky when you want to eat?'

My dining room at Burlington Lodge also provided my first opportunity for entertaining, and I was keen that the room should encourage people to enjoy themselves by creating a feeling of warmth and intimacy. I covered the walls with a huge variety of paintings, prints, posters and drawings, decorated the window with swags of hops, and stood daisy trees underneath to make an arch of foliage. An upright piano stood in a corner. Lighting is one of the easiest ways to alter the mood of any room and I have always loved dining by candle light – it enhances the food and the guests, not to mention the host – so when I was given a nineteenth-century chandelier, I returned it to its original de-electrified state and filled it with candles.

In my dining room at Battersea, the initial impression was of a far more uncluttered, modern interior than the one at Burlington Lodge, even though much of the furniture was antique. This effect was largely created by the way in which the furniture was arranged, and illustrates how adaptable, and deceptively modern, traditional furniture can be. Among the most striking objects in the room were four large mahogany bookcases, circa 1810, discovered in a cellar in a state of extreme dilapidation. Fortunately, while they were being repaired the restorer discovered a scrap of the original fabric used to line the lower open shelves and the doors of the upper sections, which we were able to match exactly. The bookcases were originally made to be fitted into a library, some arranged continuously along a wall, others filling the space between windows. By standing them apart from one another they created a very different, but no less imposing effect. In between we placed two pedestals – one antique, one a modern replica – and a pair of Japanese cloisonne lamps.

The table, which was made over 170 years later by Linley, circa 1986, was made for my father-in-law's house, Baynton, in Wiltshire. I remember that when Lord Petersham

(opposite) The dining area of our apartment in Battersea was boldly furnished with a walnut table made by Linley for my father-in-law. His primary specification when he commissioned the table was that it should be strong enough for him to dance an Irish jig on. The bookcases behind were discovered in a state of disrepair and restored to their former glory. The fabric lining the panels of brass lattice was carefully matched to a fragment of the original we found clinging to one of the doors.

came into the shop to discuss the table, this represented an important (and very welcome) commission for the business. He had no particular preference as far as style was concerned but he did make one rather unusual stipulation: the table had to be strong enough for him to dance an Irish jig on. With this in mind we constructed it from solid walnut – fourteen trees' worth – rather than the more usual veneered style. Several years later when I started visiting Serena at Baynton I was alarmed to see that the table's lacquer surface had been damaged by water. After trying and failing to polish the marks away I removed the table and had it French polished to give it its present lustrous surface. By the time we moved to Battersea, Lord Petersham had sold Baynton and moved to Yorkshire, and no longer had room for the table.

We, meanwhile, had a large space to fill, so we were delighted when he offered it to us. The huge, beautifully figured surface allows plenty of room for extravagant centrepieces of flowers, fruit and candles, all of which have helped to create some memorable dinners – without the need to dance a jig.

 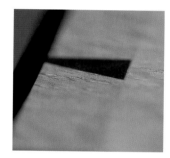

Panelling in a dining room invariably makes it feel warm and convivial, and there's a marvellous example in Sir Ambrose Heal's house. I like the fact that the room is simple rather than overly rustic, and the plain damask tablecloth seems to complement perfectly the darkness of the oak.

In complete contrast to the rich, warm colours of traditional dining rooms are the bold, uncluttered interiors shown opposite and on pp98–99. In both of these rooms simple arrangements and pared-down colour schemes have resulted in striking yet extremely practical dining rooms in which to entertain. Both rooms have tables, matching sideboards and chairs made by Linley. In the first, the American black walnut table is veneered in a simple diamond parquetry design, but the strong impression given by the furniture and paintings is softened by the blue upholstered chairs. In the second, similarly stream-lined room, designed by Kelly Hoppen, a monochrome colour scheme of black, white and natural shades is reflected both in the structure of the room – a plain wood floor and white walls – as well as in the furnishings and decorative elements. This dining table is also made from American black walnut with burr wood in the centre panel and ebony banding, and matches the sideboards which have black granite tops – a practical surface for serving food – and drawers for cutlery. Despite the

(opposite) Two huge paintings by Stephen Conroy provide an unusual focal point in this striking contemporary dining room. The table and side cabinets were made by Linley from American black walnut veneered in a parquetry design and inlaid with ebony stringing to reflect the strong black accents of the paintings. The chairs upholstered in blue damask add a softer note to the powerful overall impact of this arrangement.
(above) Details showing the traditional dove tail construction of the drawers and the contrasting grains of rich walnut and ebony.

simplicity of the room, there are numerous unusual details that add interest. The walnut-turned handles have silver centres, the walls are hung with clusters of white seals arranged in black frames, while the sideboard is decorated with lead jardinieres filled with ears of wheat.

One of the wittiest dining rooms I know is that belonging to Stephen Bayley. Furniture is kept to a minimum; there's not much apart from a plain table, bent wood chairs and a cluster of armchairs in front of the fireplace. There are no pictures on the walls and no carpets on the polished wood floor. Nevertheless, the room neatly avoids a feeling of barrenness because of a multiplicity of objects ranged along one wall. Shelves formed like toothpicks taper in thickness as they span the wall and continue on the far side of the fireplace, providing an unusual showcase for an eclectic mix of both decorative and functional objects. Alongside bundles of candles and chopsticks are morsels of sculpture, a complicated candelabra made from wire and wine bottles that looks as if it has come out of a mad scientist's laboratory, a box of silver cutlery, glasses, teacups, books, a painting, and much more besides. I'm sure that everything here tells a story or performs a function, and viewed together, like some expansive still life, it all brings a touch of quirkiness to the room.

Far more traditional in its choice of rich colour and mellow light is the dining room at Alidad's central London flat. The walls in this room are covered in hand-painted leather, a traditional wall covering for dining rooms since the late seventeenth century. It is thought to have been popular because unlike tapestry, which was used in other rooms, it didn't hold the smell of food. In this instance, the combination of leather, candles and a large mirror over the chimney piece brings a wonderful sense of richness and warmth to the room.

A far simpler interpretation of the traditional dining room, designed by John McCall, is entirely furnished with elegant eighteenth- and nineteenth-century pieces. Walls covered in a thickly woven bottle-green fabric provide a textured contrast to the rich, dark sheen of the mahogany breakfast table, and an effective background for the oil paintings in their bright, gilded frames. Further texture is added by the black upholstery of the Regency chairs.

In his London flat, Hugh Henry has given the traditional dining room a contemporary twist by paring down colour and mingling unusual objects with more traditional antiques. An eighteenth-century mahogany table is set against black leather

(opposite) Nina Campbell's dining room is arranged for maximum versatility. When not in use for dining the room doubles as a study. The walls are painted an unusual damson shade and lined with bookcases interspersed with contrasting panels painted with Roman-style grotesques. The mahogany table is by Linley and the chairs are upholstered in a bold striped fabric that echoes the colour of the walls.

upholstered chairs, which though traditional in style, thus appear modern. Above the elegant grey marble fireplace, beautifully carved with fish scales and foliage, is a painting by Sarah Armstrong Jones in similarly soft shades of grey. Dotted around the room, various striking objects draw your eye. There is a huge African drum in front of the mirror to summon guests to the table, and beside it an African headrest. Subtle lighting softens the overall effect. The standard light to the left of the chimney piece has a paper shade formed from a sequence of tetragonal shapes. As well as providing visual interest, this gives off a warm yellow light which is softly reflected by a heavily distressed mirror hanging above the sideboard.

(opposite) Stephen Bayley's generously proportioned dining room, where a plain white colour scheme and simple furniture offset an eclectic assortment of objects ranged over three shelves that stretch the length of the room.
(right) The shelves offer a useful place to store necessities alongside intriguing objets trouvés: cutlery mingles with packets of chopsticks, while pencils and books are clustered with bottles, boxes and a colourful flower painting.

One of the most adaptable examples of a dining room is Nina Campbell's. Cleverly furnished to double as a study or living area during the day, Nina has painted the walls a rather unusual plum colour. The room is lined with classical designs and bookcases, and the furniture is an harmonious mixture of old and new. The striped fabric on the Regency chairs picks up the colour of the walls, while the modern circular pedestal table provides an ideal surface for dining, working or playing.

It all goes to show that however you use them, dining rooms are far from obsolete ❖

(both pages) Details of some of the varied objects grouped as carefully as a still life on the shelves in Stephen Bayley's dining room. As your eye lingers over a pyramid of tin plate cars, a clay bust or an oval box, you cannot help wondering at the story behind each object.

(both pages) The three shelves were inspired by tooth picks: thicker at one end, tapering to a point at the other.

(both pages) Among the paraphernalia ranged on the shelves, some objects such as a cluster of cutlery, gilded glasses, a pile of church candles and a porcelain coffee cup have practical relevance to dining. Others such as the classical low-relief cast and the pair of plaster locusts are here simply because of their intriguing appearance.

With its simple arrangement of country furniture, the oak beamed and panelled dining room of Sir Ambrose Heal's home embodies traditional charm. Most of the furniture including the dining table and the chairs with trellis splats were designed by Sir Ambrose Heal in an appropriately rustic style to match the panelling. A similar table was designed for Sir Winston Churchill's house, Chartwell.

(both pages) A tour de force of
traditional design, the dining room of
this London house is adorned with a
dramatic dark green fabric on the walls
which has been carefully finished with
a ribbed binding. The use of fabric
adds a note of warmth to the overall
ambience and the dark colour contrasts
with the white marble chimney piece,
a French clock and pair of porcelain
plates on the mantelpiece, silverware
on the table and the gilded picture
frames. The circular table brings an
intimate feeling to the room and is
complemented by mahogany chairs
upholstered in black horse hair. Low
key lighting is supplied by picture
lights and candles.

(both pages) Hugh Henry has adopted
a far from traditional arrangement
in his dining room. To add richness
and an unusual element a vast leather
African drum is superimposed on a
distressed mirror and displayed on
the sideboard, which also serves as a
storage place for crockery. The antique
mahogany table displays a
contemporary stoneware vase, while
behind an unusual faceted paper lamp
provides soft indirect lighting.

(both pages) A strong uncluttered feel and fusion of old and new characterises this dining room design by Kelly Hoppen. The table and sideboard were made by Linley from American black walnut with ebony stringing and burr walnut panels. The muted tones of the upholstery, curtains and plain white walls throw the plain wood floor and furniture into dramatic relief. A Venetian mirror and a crystal chandelier add touches of tradition, while on either side of the fireplace montages of plaster seals in plain ebony frames provide accents of contrast. At the other end of the room classical-style troughs filled with neatly ranked ears of wheat stand on the sideboard.

Chapter 4 Cooking

IF AN EIGHTEENTH-CENTURY GENTLEMAN COULD VISIT A HOUSE OF
TODAY, OR GLANCE THROUGH A BOOK OF INTERIORS, HE WOULD
PROBABLY THROW UP HIS HANDS IN HORROR AT THE IMPORTANCE
ACCORDED TO THE MODERN KITCHEN.

(opposite) A collection of antique rummers and decanters ranged in a glass-fronted cabinet makes an appropriate feature in the kitchen of an art connoisseur.

(opposite) Designed by Anouska Hempel, this kitchen in a New York apartment was inspired by Beidermeier design. The cupboard doors are made from ripple birch inlaid with bands of ebony which picks up the colour of the black marble work top. Splash backs are made of mirrored glass, increasing the feeling of depth. All the appliances are steel or chrome, and even the door leading into the room has been veneered to match the cupboards.

In large houses of two hundred years ago, the functions performed by everyday appliances such as the refrigerator, freezer, cooker and dishwasher required a lengthy suite of rooms, including larders, sculleries, pantries, dairies, ice houses and butteries. The division between the domestic arrangements of a house and its so-called 'superior rooms' was staunchly guarded. Kitchens were tucked away out of sight, rarely visited by guests, who would certainly not have dreamed of eating in them. Until the late eighteenth century they were, as a rule, smoke-filled, sparsely furnished rooms, with little more than trestle tables, a couple of chairs and numerous hooks and shelves on which to store and suspend crockery and pots.

By the nineteenth century the kitchen was becoming increasingly important. In *The Doctor*, Robert Southey adds a distinctive sprinkling of romance to his description of the Yorkshire kitchen of Dr Daniel Dove: 'As you entered the kitchen there was on the right one of those open chimneys which afford more comfort in a winter's evening than the finest register stove; in front of the chimney stood a wooden bee-hive chair, and on each side was a long oak seat with a back to it, the seats serving as chests in which the oaten bread was kept. They were of the darkest brown and well polished by constant use. On the back of each were the same initials as those over the door, with the date 1610 . . . The chimney was well hung with bacon, the rack which covered half the ceiling bore equal marks of plenty; mutton hams were suspended from other parts of the ceiling; and there was an odour of cheese from the adjoining dairy . . . '

Since then the kitchen's status in the hierarchy of the house has continued to rise, and has never been higher than it is today. Most of us now view the kitchen as the heart of the house – the room to which everyone automatically gravitates. Stylistically, modern kitchens are endlessly varied. They can be elegant, efficient, spacious or compact, merely a functional place in which to cook, a family retreat, or a room in which to concoct delicious meals and entertain all at once. They also present a baffling number of choices. Where our forebears had only coal or charcoal fires and ovens on which to roast, boil, stew and bake, we now have an endless assortment of gadgets, ranging from the high-tech to the traditional, from which to choose. Perhaps a time traveller from the past might think it rather ironic that with so much technology at our disposal, one of the most enduringly popular of ovens – the Aga – has scarcely altered in appearance since its invention in the 1920s.

My own interest in cooking developed rather late in life when, having left home,

I was forced by hunger to learn some basic skills. Since then I have realised how enjoyable kitchens and cooking can be. In my apartment in Battersea I designed a kitchen with entertaining in mind; somewhere that would be both practical yet a pleasurable place in which to eat. The room was divided in two: the eating area, with a large Victorian table and chairs, was divided from the cooking area by an island which dropped down in the middle to encourage people to talk to you while cooking. The overall design reflected my fondness for blending traditional and modern elements. In this case I used many traditional materials in a very simple way to highlight the contrasting effects of their natural textures and colours. The pale limestone floor was a foil for the rich colour of the cherry wood cupboards. Cherry wood is a timber that has been used for country furniture for centuries and darkens to a beautiful warm colour with age.

On simple furniture designs it is astonishing how small details, such as the choice of a moulding or handle on a cupboard door, can transform the look of a design. Here I designed and positioned the handles myself to add a personal touch to the doors. The work surface was also extremely traditional – it was made from teak, an incredibly hard-wearing practical timber. The wood was left unsealed and needed oiling once a week to keep it well 'fed' and looking good.

In order to disguise the usual unsightly paraphernalia – toasters, blenders, sugar, tea and so on – we included what I called 'a garage', a roll-top door which came down to the work surface and hid everything away. Apart from 'the garage', all the wall cupboards had glass fronts. This not only made finding whatever you needed easier, it also encouraged you to be tidy. The sink with a brushed nickel tap was put in the traditional position under the west facing window. In order to filter the sunlight, which could be blinding by mid-afternoon, we installed a stained pine blind that clattered rather appealingly in the breeze when the window was open.

Lighting in a kitchen can be problematic, particularly if you intend to entertain in it. How do you reconcile the need for bright light to cook by and softer light for eating? In this kitchen we used halogen down lighters on different circuits so they could be switched on and off to change the atmosphere.

Just like any other room in the house, kitchens are invariably a reflection of their owners. But whereas entrance halls, dining rooms and living rooms are often showpiece rooms, kitchens usually reveal the occupant's true personality. For instance,

(opposite) In the kitchen of our apartment in Battersea we aimed to create a room that would work well as somewhere to both cook and entertain. To increase the feeling of unity we dropped the height of the central section of work top so that you could talk across the saucepans, thus whoever was cooking would feel less separate from the eating area. The cupboards were made from American cherry, with an oiled teak work top.

in Eddie and Miranda Lim's kitchen, the Aga, country table and chairs, uneven limestone floor, open shelving and unfitted open-sided units all contribute to create the epitome of a warm, sunny, traditional country kitchen. But professional equipment such as the highly efficient steamer and high-tech electric oven occasionally interrupt nostalgia and provide a large hint as to Eddie's occupation: a professional chef.

My father's kitchen in his London home is traditional with characteristic touches. A huge and highly impractical chandelier positioned over the table reflects the fact that he has never been interested in cooking, but loves to sit for hours around a table chatting. The chandelier has candlesticks in the outer sconces and an electric down lighter in the middle and is suspended from the bedroom floor above on a band of silk so that it can be raised and lowered according to the mood he wants to create. At the back of the kitchen are various traditional cupboards, including a spice cupboard that he bought some years ago from a Chinese medicine shop, all of which are painted green to match the rest of the room.

The kitchen designed by Phillip Wagner and John McCall for an art connoisseur reveals the owner's penchant for antiques and classical antiquity. The brilliant blue background of paintings inspired by Roman mosaics is complemented by strongly patterned blue tablecloths and glass. A wonderful selection of eighteenth- and nineteenth-century rummers is stored in the kitchen cabinet. Partly set in a conservatory, subtle green paintwork provides a gentle transition between garden and interior.

At the heart of Sir Ambrose Heal's country kitchen, a traditional Swedish wood-burning stove, a pair of simple ladder-back chairs, and cupboards and shelves painted a soft green point to this great designer's interest in Arts and Crafts furniture and vernacular furnishing styles. An unusual decorative focal point is provided by the stove chimney, clad in attractive blue and white tiles.

A similarly personal kitchen is to be found in the London home of a retired diplomat. The owner's newfound passion for photography is reflected in beautiful scenes of Skye which echo the blue and white china housed in open racks beneath them. Elsewhere, on mirror-backed glass shelving are an exquisite assortment of Venetian glass, silver and ceramics, while a cramped corner provides a space for an ingenious wine rack.

Ann Boyd has opted for a more modern, pared-down approach. Within a relatively small space she manages to convey a sense of calm by banishing all clutter and sticking

(opposite) The eating area in the kitchen designed by John McCall for an art connoisseur is dominated by two bold collages made from layers of tissue paper depicting classical heads by Riccardo Cinalli. Strongly patterned fabrics are layered over the table adding further accents of brilliant blue. The soft greenish white of the walls acts as a subtle link between the kitchen and the garden.

(above) My father's London kitchen is simply furnished and dominated by a large chandelier. Although this may not be the obvious choice of lighting for a kitchen it has proved surprisingly successful. By a clever arrangement of ropes and pulleys the height can be adjusted according to the mood he wishes to create – usually up during lunch and down during dinner.

firmly to a strict all-white colour scheme in her choice of cupboards, tiles and marble work top. An intimate, feminine and highly personal touch is provided by a few well-positioned pieces of blue and white pottery, with silver plates standing behind and glass bowls arranged with different fruits.

In Stephen Bayley's kitchen a similar pared-down look is interestingly combined with tradition. Alongside all the modern gadgets and metal surfaces is a traditional ceramic pot sink and a nice array of glass jars that remind me of a country dresser.

Although white is well suited to basement kitchens, the danger is that it can look cold and harsh. In the kitchen opposite, this pit-fall is neatly avoided by using two shades of off-white for the units and contrasting them with a black granite work top and a dark polished wood floor. These subtleties give the room an understated softness that is continued with an attractive display of country pottery on the top of the cupboards.

The problem of storage is of course always a thorny one in any kitchen, especially if space is restricted. I noticed one unusual way of overcoming this problem on a visit to interior designer Hugh Henry's flat. In between a display of atmospheric black and white photographs he had arranged his knives, sieves, scissors, bottle openers and a scoop on pins on the wall, as carefully as works of art. Another way to solve this problem is to fill every available inch of space with cupboards, as in the kitchen of the New York apartment designed by Anouska Hempel for a Swedish financier. The result is a warm, uncluttered, highly sophisticated interior, with a polished pine floor, cupboards made from ripple-figured birch inlaid with ebony, and a black marble surface. Notice that the space between the wall and base cupboards is mirrored to add depth and light, and even the kitchen door matches the rest of the cupboards.

Finally, an antithesis to fitted kitchens is the eclectically assembled example found in my friend Greg Powlesland's cottage in Cornwall. I first got to know Greg when he was my tutor at Parnham. A multi-talented man who sculpts, designs and paints, Greg delights in salvaging and bartering for anything that might come in handy. Thus, in his kitchen he has installed cupboards made from reclaimed doors, a vintage ceramic sink and taps, and a draining board fashioned from slabs of black slate. Slate shelving also provides somewhere to show off an attractive collection of vintage carved breadboards. With its unstudied, welcoming and relaxed atmosphere this is undoubtedly one of the most personal and idiosyncratic kitchens I know ❖

(opposite) Nostalgic clutter combines with high-tech simplicity in this basement kitchen. The cupboards, hand-painted in two soft shades of white, are in a simple traditional style. The work top, made from black slate, adds a cool, rather modern note which is countered by the warmth provided by a floor of varnished wood. A feeling of unaffected simplicity is introduced by the simple metal chairs and the table with its brightly chequered cloth. At the far end of the room a dresser cupboard crammed with crockery and bottles is a subtle reminder of traditional country dressers.

(left) Ceramics are a delightful way in which to introduce splashes of colour to a kitchen. In this example white cupboards provide a perfect foil for a varied collection of flowery plates, a tin box and a heart-shaped dish.
(below) The coolness of slate made it a popular alternative to marble for shelving in traditional pantries and larders, and it has recently enjoyed a revival in the most modern of kitchens. It is a lustrous material that looks wonderful when seen, as here, next to stainless steel. The advantage of a work top such as this is that the draining board can be cut into the work top, providing a clean, uncluttered look.

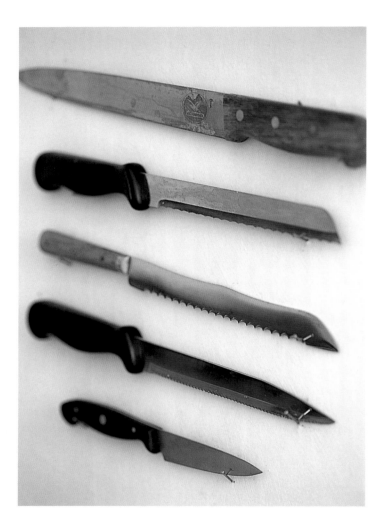

(both pages) The unpretentious galley kitchen of designer Hugh Henry's London flat has an uncluttered feel about it, although it contains everything you need for food preparation. An L-shaped range of kitchen cupboards provides ample storage space as well as a work surface on which containers and gadgets are ranged. Many of the most frequently used utensils are attached to the wall where they also serve as an unusual decorative feature. I can't help feeling, though, that this would be great when you needed to quickly grab something, but more tricky when it came to putting them away again.

The ceilings in this tiny kitchen are unusually high and provide a perfect space on which to display an imposing set of black and white photographs.

(below) The kitchen is unusually lit with a metal ceiling lantern which also acts as a visual link between the black framed photographs.

(left) At first sight you could be forgiven for thinking that this sunny yellow kitchen belongs in a country farmhouse. The uneven limestone floor, the Aga nestling amid wooden cupboards and an old-fashioned plate rack give Miranda and Eddie Lim's kitchen an air of traditional charm. Look more closely, however, and you will notice the kitchen also contains the most up-to-date of appliances.

(below) A vast stainless steel steamer that looks as if it belongs in a laboratory is fitted into one of the cupboards. Some interesting personal touches add to the homely feel: the tiles behind the range were arranged by Eddie, and there is an attractive antique ceiling light suspended over the table to offer a softer alternative to the down lighters illuminating other parts of the room.

In a converted cart shed, a centrepiece of Sir Ambrose Heal's house is this attractive Swedish ceramic wood-burning stove. The flue is clad in blue and white tiles, while the chimney breast behind is inset with panels of Deutscher Werkbund tiles depicting various animals. To either side fitted shelves and cupboards epitomise Sir Ambrose Heal's delight in traditional craftsmanship and materials.

(left) Black granite work tops provide a strong contrast to the simple white painted cupboards in Juliet and Robert Hardman's kitchen. A white Aga placed under a chimney forms the centrepiece of the units. The eating area is clearly divided from the rest of the kitchen by drawers and open shelves set at right angles to the wall. Chairs covered in white add a note of formal elegance to the overall effect.

(right) Stephen Bayley opts for a more industrial appearance in his kitchen using wood work tops and floor, grey metal cupboards and plain white tiles to create the desired effect. Nevertheless, vestiges of tradition linger on. Centred beneath the window at the far end is a traditional white ceramic pot sink, while open shelves overflow with jars of culinary delicacies.

(both pages) There is an appealing sturdiness and lack of pretension about Greg Powlesland's kitchen. Most of what you can see has been bartered, swapped or reclaimed. Slabs of Cornish slate are used as shelves and echoed in the strong slate blue wall behind and painted panels in the cupboard on the right. An old kelim creates an ingenious screen for the untidy clutter underneath the sink. Many of the antiques dotted about the kitchen are used for their original purpose as well as for decoration. A wonderful old copper kettle sitting on the Aga still functions as effectively as when it was first made.

(both pages) A carefully arranged display of glass instills light, elegance and jewel-like brilliance in even the gloomiest corners of a kitchen. Here, a collection of Murano glass is used to striking effect. Deep blue goblets are ranged on glass shelves with mirrors set behind to make them seem doubly imposing. Elsewhere there are tumblers with spiralling canes of blue-on-white, and white-on-blue, gilded and fluted glasses, and glass bowls decorated with roundels of contrasting coloured glass.

(both pages) Ann Boyd's kitchen strikes a subtle balance with a clean, clinical look softened by a few carefully selected pieces of pottery. Blue and white meat platters are arranged on a high shelf; below on open stainless steel shelves fitted round the cooker hood are an attractive assortment of blue and white jugs. Opposite, the white work top and cupboards provide a perfect foil for silver plates and glass bowls brimming with vividly coloured fruits.

'EVERY MAN,' DECLARED DR JOHNSON, EXTOLLING THE VIRTUES OF
A GOOD LETTER-WRITER, 'SHOULD WISH TO BE ABLE TO GIVE DELIGHT
AT A DISTANCE.' JOHNSON'S SENTIMENT WAS FAR FROM ORIGINAL –
MERELY A TESTIMONY TO THE PREVAILING PASSION FOR LETTER-
WRITING REFLECTED IN A DAZZLING VARIETY OF WRITING AND
LIBRARY FURNITURE FORMS THAT EVOLVED IN THE EIGHTEENTH
CENTURY.

(opposite) Architectural restraint is the
keynote of this handsome eighteenth-
century Scandinavian bureau bookcase
that forms a centrepiece of the study in
Hugh Henry's flat. Furniture such as
this appeals to me greatly for the way
in which practicality seemlessly
combines with elegance. The upper
cupboards might hide a jumble of
papers and writing paraphernalia, but
once the doors are closed no one would
know it. Below, a plethora of small
drawers and compartments provide yet
more storage space; the circular
compartments are particularly unusual
and make a nice contrast with the
rectangular shapes. A white bust
flanked by two ceramic vases adds
extra height and complements the
white shades of the lamps below. In the
centre is a witty touch: a blotter, ink
stand and quill.

Bureaux, writing desks, secretaires, writing tables in a multiplicity of sizes and shapes, all testify to the burgeoning popularity of letter-writing. Reading had enjoyed a similarly meteoric escalation in popularity and the century is equally rich in library tables, desks, chairs, ingenious metamorphic library steps which could turn into stools, and vastly ornate bookcases festooned with carving or built in the form of Greek or Roman temples, to mirror the architecture of the room.

The emergence of all this furniture was also a result of the enormous popularity of rooms devoted to the pursuits of reading and writing – the library or study. This was a significant departure from the early seventeenth century, when collections of books were a rarity in private houses. An inventory of Hardwick Hall made in 1601 reveals that Bess of Hardwick, the richest woman in England after the Queen, possessed only six books which she kept in her bed chamber. As books became more widely available, a study or library became an essential in many homes. The diarist Samuel Pepys wrote proudly of the hours he took to organise his collection of books in 1668: 'Up and to my chamber, where all the morning making a catalogue of my books; which did find me work, but with great pleasure, my chamber and books being now set in very good order and my chamber washed and cleaned . . . ' and goes on to recall that after dinner he had his head combed (for lice presumably) 'and then to my chamber and read most of the evening till pretty late'. A century and a half later, in Jane Austen's *Pride and Prejudice*, the much put-upon Mr Bennet frequently retreats to his library when the romantic shenanigans of his daughters become too much for him.

Like the bewildered Mr Bennet I also believe that the essence of a study is that it should provide a private preserve, a personal sanctuary rather than a showcase room, where one can escape to read, write or contemplate and be sheltered from the rest of the world. This notion was doubtless born from the first study I remember – my father's. Unfortunately the room no longer exists, so I can't include a photograph of it. In contrast to the traditional mahogany furnishings with which the eighteenth- and nineteenth-century gentleman would have been familiar, it was for its day (the 1960s) an extraordinarily avant-garde interior, furnished with plain Douglas fir floorboards, white walls, metal rack shelving that ran from floor to ceiling, and a very simple desk that he had made himself from wood, leather and metal tubing welded together. At the time, my father was working as a researcher for B&W, and so the room also included a state of the art hi-fi system with countless shiny knobs and vast speakers.

(opposite) A library designed by Anouska Hempel for a Swedish financier in early nineteenth-century Russian style. The cabinets, made by Linley from mahogany with ebony inlay and ivory substitute, were inspired by eighteenth-century quill boxes. Walls are panelled to match in solid ebony with bands of mahogany inset. The harder you look at this room the more you marvel at its extraordinary attention to detail – even the returns of the windows have been carefully considered: they are faced with mirrors to amplify the light in the room.

The study belonging to my friend Greg Powlesland is to my mind every bit as characteristic of its owner as I remember my father's to have been, albeit in a totally different style. It is a room in which Greg writes, draws, designs and reads, and everything in it is a reflection of his interests. The chair, held together with bits of string, he made himself. Displayed around the room are balls of twine, pebbles, models of ships, and his own carvings. On the wall is a photograph of a Camper & Nicholson gentleman's racing yacht which has particular significance for me. I remember that while I was at Parnham House he invited me to the Isle of Wight to rescue a yacht that he'd heard about. We found the yacht lying derelict on a beach about to be burned. After paying £40 for it, we spent the night outside on deck, waiting until 3am for the tide to come up so that we could remove it. Greg spent the next fifteen years working on it, and as this photo shows, has now restored it to its former glory.

Interior designer Hugh Henry's study has a similarly masculine atmosphere, although it is far more sparingly furnished. Hugh spends much of his time working from home: the painting on the desk is a design for a carpet. I love the fact that there is nothing superfluous here, and yet the room is not intimidatingly ordered. There's an appealing jumble in the bookcase (although I hate to think what would happen if you tried to pull a book out from the bottom) and the spines of the books and the figures standing in front of them give vivid splashes of colour to the otherwise restrained colour scheme. If there's one thing I covet in this room it's the bureau-cabinet. To me, this epitomises fine cabinetmaking: simple and elegant, with interesting features such as the circular form of the two central drawers.

The study of the London house on p132 has a Linley desk containing three secret drawers. Ever since my grandmother showed me the desk with its secret drawer I have been fascinated by furniture containing puzzles and hidden drawers and especially enjoy making desks with secret compartments. Like most of our furniture the desk is a modern interpretation of a traditional design. It is veneered in mahogany – a popular wood for writing furniture – and the flame pattern is a result of cutting the veneers from the join between two branches.

The study designed by John McCall for an art connoisseur reflects a far more formal and traditional approach to the gentleman's study. This is a study in which Mr Bennet might have felt at home, since there is hardly anything here (apart from the electric lights) that would not have been present in a Regency gentleman's day.

(opposite) One of the shelves in Greg Powlesland's study showing the photograph of the Camper & Nicholson racing yacht he painstakingly restored. The oak leaf dates from our college days when we all had to carve a leaf as an exercise. Beneath is a beautifully crafted nineteenth-century ship's model of the Marigold.

The rather serious ambience is partly a result of the strictly symmetrical arrangement of the furniture. In the centre of the room a leather-topped library table provides a generous surface for writing and reading. On either side are two Regency klismos chairs, upholstered in horsehair and traditionally studded with brass pins. There are identical chimney pieces at both ends of the room, each bordered by bookcases recessed into niches. At one end the shelves are concealed behind glazed doors filled with fabric – a good way to hide unsightly clutter. In front, on either side of the hearth, are a pair of traditional library chairs and a foot stool. The mirrored panels framing the fireplace which reflect the bookshelves at the other end are an innovative touch. The dark red colour of the walls gives a warm glow to the room and you can just imagine losing track of time seated in front of the fire with a good book.

The library of Bill Blass's New York apartment evokes a similar sense of formality and tradition. With its central circular table and wonderful collection of leather-bound books, porcelain, sculpture and antique cabinetmaker's models, this too is very much a showcase room for a connoisseur collector.

The library in the New York apartment on pp140–141, designed by Anouska Hempel, has a rather unusual Russian theme, which relates to its owner's upbringing. Much of the furniture in this room, including the table, two large mahogany cabinets with ebony inlay, and the matching ebony and mahogany panelling, was commissioned from Linley. A set of highly decorated lustreware plates add richness to the effect of so much dark wood. The new furniture has been designed to echo the antique Empire-style pieces. The overall effect is of a timeless classicism that is never going to seem outdated.

The room designed by Greg Jordan on pp135–136 is cozy but far less formal. This is a room in which to chat and relax with a drink, as well as read; there is a bar conveniently placed alongside the bookcase. I love this room for its bold use of contrasting colours. Dark blue walls throw the cream chimney surround into dramatic relief, and there's a clever mixture of patterns which all add warmth to the room. The room is also filled with a wonderfully personal assortment of unusual decorative objects: there are vases of antique metal flowers, assorted silver-mounted horn cups and treen objects, including a tall turned candlestick, dotted about the room. Even the tartan used to upholster a chair, and that on the chest which serves as a coffee table, has family associations.

(opposite) Perfectly positioned beneath a window, the desk in this London study was made by Linley based on a traditional knee-hole design. The drawer fronts are faced with flame-figured mahogany with ebony beading. From a furniture designer's point of view, one of the most appealing aspects about desks is that they lend themselves particularly well to secret compartments: this example has three.

In Princess Salimah Aga Khan's London home, one end of a large drawing room has been furnished as a study with a beautiful mahogany architect's table that serves as a multi-functional desk. The table was made in the early nineteenth century by Gillows of Lancaster and operates by a complex system of ratchets that allows the top flap to rise at an angle or flat. I remember designing a similar folding desk when I was at college, and spending hours on working out how to create such a system. It was only later that I discovered that Gillows had beaten me to it by more than a century and a half. The top of the architect's table also provides an effective surface on which to display writing materials. A collection of pens is ranged on a cast iron stand next to

(right) Architect's table, made by leading furniture makers Gillows of Lancaster c.1810. I have always been fascinated by mechanical furniture, and in particular pieces such as this which combine elegance with novelty. The trompe l'oeil picture above, by the Dutch artist Evert Collier, depicts a letter rack.

(opposite) The study of an upstate New York home designed by Greg Jordan. Bold printed fabrics and deep colours help to create a sense of welcoming intimacy that makes this a comfortable room in which to chat with friends as well as study in solitude. Against the dark walls notes of contrast are supplied by the cream-coloured chimney piece and lamp shades; a floral patterned needlepoint rug is also coordinated to match. A tartan trunk covered with a sheet of glass forms an ingenious coffee table.

assorted quills and blotters. Above is an early eighteenth-century trompe l'oeil by the Dutch artist Evert Collier, showing a letter rack on which a miniature of Charles I is suspended. Pamphlets, a pen knife, a seal, wax and a quill are also threaded into the board; no picture could better encapsulate the charms of a study ❖

(below) The mantelpiece arranged by Greg Jordan displays an eclectic assortment of decorative pieces. Vases filled with tall columns of metal flowers add height, and beside is another vase filled with white fern leaves and rosebuds. Ranged in between are a collection of silver-mounted horn drinking cups.

(opposite) Vibrant red walls and boldly patterned curtains lend an air of grandeur to this formal library designed by John McCall for a typical London town house. The far wall is arranged with rigorous attention to detail: bookcases have been built into the recesses on either side of the chimney breast, and above the chimney piece the wall has been softened with the addition of mouldings and inset glass panelling. In the foreground a large library table provides a generous surface for letter writing or studying.

(both pages) Bill Blass's elegant library is arranged around a large circular nineteenth-century Viennese table with a chamfered stand. The fabric used to upholster the chair seats cleverly reflects this form with classical figures framed in a scalloped border. The neutral tones of the walls highlight the rich patina of the furniture. The walls have been divided into sections with the use of heavy mouldings. Behind the table an architectural model of a rotunda stands on a side table with a stand carved in imitation of a pile of books. Beside the recessed bookcase is an elegant flat-fronted Empire secretaire with a pair of bronze candlesticks in the form of eagles standing on top.

(left) Barriers between different parts of the room are formed by a pair of cabinets. Made from mahogany, they are mounted on ebony plinths to match the panelling, black cornicing and the ebony panels in the parquetry floor. (right) A set of six early nineteenth-century Russian chairs arranged around a library table made by Linley to match. The distinctive black and white striped fabric used to cover the chair seats is echoed elsewhere in the apartment and complements a rug hand-painted in a strong geometric design.

(opposite) In designer Hugh Henry's study an informal ambience is provided by the hectic arrangement of books in the bookcase and three amusing clown figures standing in front. As elsewhere in the flat, neutral walls accentuate the textures of decorative objects such as a pair of mineral specimen lamps.
(below) A sloped artist's table positioned underneath the window provides a useful space for drawing and painting designs such as this one for a rug.

(left) Greg Powlesland's down-to-earth study contains a simple nineteenth-century mahogany table and a large mahogany bureau. Surfaces overflow with objects that have caught Greg's eye for one reason or another. A bowl of rough textured pebbles strikes an interesting contrast to a stack of books and a wooden draught board.

(below) Shelves not only serve as storage for books and files but also as somewhere to display stone carvings and a wedding photo. The whale's tail carving is a reminder of the time Greg spent in Iceland when he became fascinated by the wildlife of the region.

A PEACEFUL SANCTUARY, A PRIVATE RETREAT, SOMEWHERE TO RELAX;
MOST PEOPLE WOULD PROBABLY AGREE THAT A BEDROOM SHOULD
PROVIDE ALL OF THESE, AS WELL AS SOMEWHERE TO SLEEP. FROM OUR
TWENTY-FIRST CENTURY VIEWPOINT IT COMES AS SOMETHING OF A
SURPRISE, THEREFORE, TO DISCOVER THAT THESE NOTIONS OF A
BEDROOM ARE RELATIVELY NEWBORN.

(opposite) Subtle colours accentuate the richness of the furnishings in this masculine bedroom designed by John McCall. A pair of lamps on obelisk bases flank an extravagantly gilded and crested antique mirror.

Olive green lamp shades form a strong link with the green patterned curtains behind. A wooden box on the dressing table provides a practical place in which to hide clutter.

Traditionally, the best bed chamber was considered on a par with other important reception rooms – as much a showroom as a saloon or dining room. In many large houses the main bedrooms were situated downstairs off a withdrawing room, with a closet or cabinet leading on for dressing and washing, as well as for holding private meetings and displaying special treasures.

The importance of the bedroom was reflected not just in its position within the layout of the house, but also in its furnishings. For centuries the bed was regarded as the most important and expensive piece of furniture, setting the tone for the decor of the room. Early inventories describe beds adorned with the most sumptuous wool, velvet, silver, gold or brocade hangings, which not only kept the occupants warm – essential in draughty houses of the day – but also gave them a modicum of privacy. The eighteenth-century diarist Fanny Burney described the King's bedroom at Knole, a typically grand state bedroom of the seventeenth century: ' . . . the third state-room was magnificence itself: it was fitted up for King William. The bed-curtains, tester, quilt, and valance were all of gold flowers, worked upon a silver ground: its value even in those days, was £7,000.'

By and large, bedrooms were not particularly private places. Servants often slept in the same room as their master, on makeshift 'truckle' beds or mattresses that were rolled away when not in use. During daylight hours bedrooms served as rooms in which privileged visitors might be received. Many were furnished with a large formal seat at the foot of the bed for the person holding audience (if he was not still propped up in bed) and a suite of chairs arranged around the wall for his visitors to sit on while they talked to him.

As the cabinetmaker's skills developed in the eighteenth century, so the furnishing styles of bedrooms became increasingly varied, ranging from restrained classical elegance to the inventive quirkiness of the Gothic and Chinese styles. Sophie la Roche, a German visitor to London in the late eighteenth century, much admired an example she saw on her travels: 'The bedroom displayed yet another aspect of the Countess's industry and good taste. It is hung with a delicate monotone pale-blue chintz, with a border of the sweetest flower garlands embroidered in blue of the same shade on a white ground, similarly the curtains, quilts on both the beds, and chair-covers. The charm and simplicity of this room are inexpressible,' she enthused after a visit to Lord Harcourt's house, Leonard's Hill in Windsor Forest. Not all bedrooms were similarly

(opposite) A vivid reminder of the opulence of seventeenth-century bed chambers, this amazingly preserved antique satin bed coverlet is embroidered with silk and metal threads in a complex crewel work design of foliage, fruit and flowers.

esteemed. At Badminton House a Chinese bedroom, furnished by John Linnell with lavish japanned furniture, Chinese wallpaper and an extraordinary pagoda-like bed, was decried by another lady critic, Lady Mary Wortley Montagu, as the ultimate in 'barbarous, gaudy gout'.

Apart from the bed, the particular requirements of the bedroom have given rise to a spectacular variety of furniture. Ladies often wrote letters in their bedrooms, thus creating a demand for fragile writing desks and boxes; bed steps made getting in and out of high beds easier; press cupboards, chests and tall boys provided storage for cloths and linen; dressing chests were often fitted out with slides for a gentleman's brushes, or a top drawer with special compartments for cosmetics; while close-stools and commodes provided discreet receptacles for the chamber pot, pre built-in plumbing.

As many of the bedrooms on the following pages testify, much antique bedroom furniture is highly versatile, as practical today as when it was first made, and can combine easily with more modern pieces. Greg Powlesland's cottage bedroom is a wonderful testimony of how easily old and new work together. His home is set above the Helford River with spectacular views from the windows. The furniture is predominately traditional Victorian mahogany, but the heaviness of the wood is given a great lift with a fantastically bright quilt made by a young artist.

Traditional furniture forms provided the inspiration for one of our most memorable commissions – a suite of furniture for a bedroom in Sir Elton John's London home. Elton has been a patron from the earliest days of the business; a vast Palladian marquetry bed was one of the first things we made for him, and in many ways marked a turning point in helping to establish our company's ability to undertake such large commissions. This room is unusual in its layout in that one wall is an open gallery leading on to the staircase. All the furniture is made from sycamore, a wood that is notoriously hard to use because its colour is so inconsistent. Combined as it is here with a bare sycamore floor it has resulted in a clean look ideally suited to the airy openness of the room and to urban living.

On the flat surfaces of the bedside cupboards, the strong ripple grain has been emphasised by cutting the veneers using a traditional method known as quartering: four slices are cut from the same piece of wood and then laid at ninety-degree angles to one another. The paleness of the sycamore is prevented from appearing bland thanks

(opposite) Detail of the bedroom in Sir Elton John's London house for which Linley supplied the furniture. The table is made of ripple sycamore, burr ash and walnut. Armchairs inspired by eighteenth-century design are given a modern touch with faux leopard-skin upholstery.

to the use of small areas of richer contrasting inlays of ebony, amboyna and walnut. The feeling of richness and sophistication is also enhanced by a collection of Art Nouveau and Art Deco vases, cleverly side lit to give a jewel-like intensity to the various colours of the glass, while the use of leopard print bedcover and cushions adds a playful touch.

Hugh Henry's bedroom is particularly ingenious; the melange of traditional furniture and unusual objects creates a highly adaptable room that can be turned from a bedroom into a living room or workroom. The restrained use of colour helps focus attention on the unusual forms and textures of the objects displayed here, as well as creating a general sense of calm that I think is essential to a successful bedroom. A traditional mahogany bed, placed against a wall so it can double as a sofa, is positioned under a collage of tools and an antique garden design. An antique specimen chest provides useful storage and a surface on which to display a pair of black contemporary vases, while a pair of modern steel lamps shine on an African mask.

In my own bedrooms I have tried to create this sense of peace using pale colours and plenty of white paint. In Burlington Lodge, my Victorian bachelor flat in Fulham, the windows were tall and long. At the time I lived there I was constantly travelling, and I recall that the room was always filled with suitcases. The leather case with the ivory brushes was intended for weekends away. The table on which it stands was one of the first console tables made by Linley. The chaise longue was designed by my great-uncle, Oliver Messel.

Although we had far more space to play with in the apartment at Battersea, our intention was to create a room that would be similarly simple, light and airy. We kept the ceiling plain, without a cornice, and made the room as light as possible by putting in two long, shuttered windows that opened on to a tiny terrace. To add interest to the flat wall, as well as provide a focal point to balance the bed, we built a chimney breast between the windows. The white marble chimney piece complemented the light, airy theme and gave me a useful surface on which to display my collection of silver-mounted coconuts from the Caribbean. One of the things I loved about the room was that everything in it told a story: I inherited the Italian commode from Oliver Messel; the marble on the side table comes from Connemara in Ireland, where my wife Serena was brought up; the bed was a wedding present from my father-in-law; I was given the icon of St George and the Dragon by my godmother. The Aubusson carpet I recovered

(opposite) The bedroom of my bachelor flat at Burlington Lodge, Fulham. I made the room as light as possible using plain white walls with white painted shutters and gauze draped over a curtain pole to create a simple swag. The side tables provided useful surfaces on which to display photographs, as well as serving as stands for the bedside lamps. The walnut chest is probably Italian and was inherited in a dilapidated state from Oliver Messel.

from the top of my father's boiler, where it had sat for three decades. When it was washed it transformed from a dirty grey to these soft shades of pink, which worked perfectly with the upholstery of the bed.

Among the most theatrical bedrooms I know are two designed by Anouska Hempel, Linley and Charles Allen for the New York apartment of a Swedish financier. The flamboyant black and white striped theme might not be to everyone's taste but it certainly has incredible visual impact – note how the vertical stripes of wall, curtains and bedcover are continued in the strong uprights of the mahogany bed. The room is exquisitely furnished with an arrangement of six Venetian mirrors and a wonderful Italian ebony cabinet against which is set a pair of richly upholstered crimson armchairs. Leading off from the master bedroom is a dressing room in which black walls and rich mahogany mirrored cupboards lend the room the air of a gentlemen's club. Adjustable lights are fitted on brass rails and add softness, while the wood floor inset with a border of black slate provides further richness. The black and white theme has been continued in the guest bedroom, where twin ebonised tester beds by Linley are hung with striped awnings and matching bedcovers, and the same pattern is continued on the walls and carpet. Again, look closely and you discover a wealth of wonderful detail: the handles on the bedside cabinet are made from mother of pearl; the strong uprights of the ebonised bedside lamps echo the bedposts; while the walls are hung with black and white architectural prints.

Equally sophisticated but far more serene and airy is the bedroom in Bill Blass's New York apartment. There are no curtains or carpets, and apart from the bed, which is upholstered in a rich paisley fabric, there is little colour in the room. The richness comes from the contrast of textures – bronze, stone, wood – and a wealth of unusual objects. Looking at the room you cannot fail to be aware that each piece of furniture and decorative element has been carefully considered, not only for its own merit but also for the way it relates to the objects surrounding it. At the far end of the room is a large fitted bookcase on which the books are carefully ranged according to size. In front, on an unusual table with carved animal legs, a collection of sculpture and objets trouvé are displayed. At the foot of the bed is a long window seat upholstered in ostrich leather.

A world away from the glossy refinement of these two New York apartments, I cannot help admiring the homely bedroom in a dower house of a large country estate. The owner of this bedroom is an elderly lady, and the charm of her room lies in the

(opposite) A dramatic and rather formal bedroom. The bold black and white fabric used for the curtains and bedcover is echoed on the walls and in the strong horizontal posts of an antique mahogany bed.

sense of living history you feel looking at the embroidered linen counterpane and eiderdown, the glove stretcher and dressing case, and the bed tray with its ingenious hinged flap that allows you to read comfortably in bed.

While both the bedrooms I have created for myself have been fairly traditional in their overall effect, I have always greatly admired the purity of the minimalist bedroom. In Stephen Bayley's bedroom there is little apart from a bed, two plain cupboards on either side and a chest and teak cabinet on the other side of the room. Despite my admiration for its total absence of clutter, I can't help wondering how he manages without somewhere to put his glass of water or a reading light!

(opposite) It is hard to imagine a more pared-down bedroom than Stephen Bayley's. Colour has been banished to focus attention on the shapes and textures of the objects in the room. Central to the simple furnishing scheme is the plain bed and two armoires set in niches on either side. On the other side of the room a teak cabinet (far right) creates a display area for a model boat, a vase of leaves and a Shaker box. (right) The monochrome theme continues on the landing with a simple cane seated bench and a muted picture hanging above.

Ann Boyd's bedroom seems to blend old and new and achieves the essence of unadorned simplicity and elegance. Storage of clothes is of course fundamental to an uncluttered bedroom. Here, Ann has confronted the problem stylishly in a very restricted space by using mirrored doors that make the room look bigger and lighter. In the bedroom proper, two faux bamboo painted chairs stand on either side of a metal-framed trestle table with a glass top on which stands a lamp and two beautiful pots. A framed mirror hangs above, a couple of storage boxes beneath. The plain white bed is reflected in the glass. There is no need for anything else ❖

(both pages) Landings in this London house designed by John McCall are furnished with as much care and attention to detail as the rooms.
(left) The landing has been fitted with bookshelves set into a recess, while the wall is used to display a set of architectural prints. A narrow mahogany table is set in front of the window to disguise a radiator.
(right) An elegant marble-topped commode displays a Chinese famille rose porcelain bowl. The bold striped blind brings a touch of warmth and is mellowed by the subtle seascape hanging beside it.

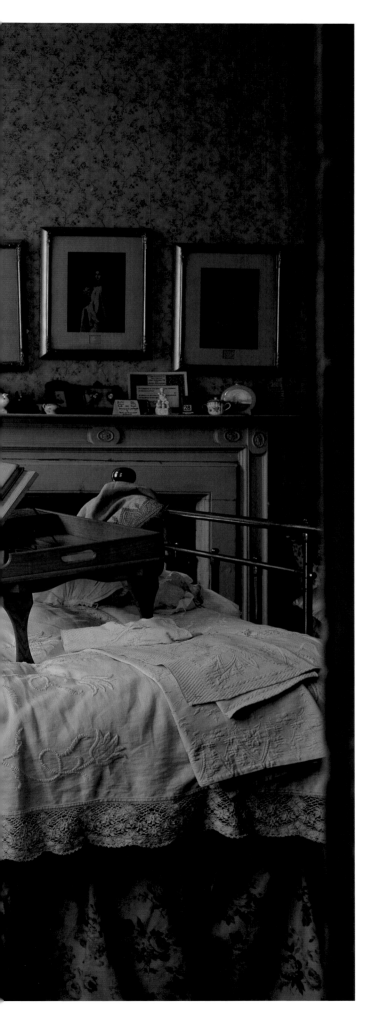

(left) A bedroom that exudes a feeling of faded grandeur. Layers of antique linen bedclothes are displayed on the nineteenth-century brass bedstead. In the foreground is a vintage travelling case, complete with brushes, bottles and a glove stretcher. In the corner behind stands a decoupage screen.

(above) Greg Powlesland's bedroom neatly combines tradition and modernity. Curtains of softly patterned chintz and a vase of country flowers form subtle counterparts for a bold nineteenth-century mahogany bed enlivened with a brilliantly-coloured quilt.

(both pages) Elegant Empire style is used in a rather restrained manner in this guest bedroom in Hugh Henry's flat. Against plain white walls the heavy wooden bed frame provides a focal point that is balanced on the opposite wall by a beautifully carved mahogany wardrobe and a library chair.

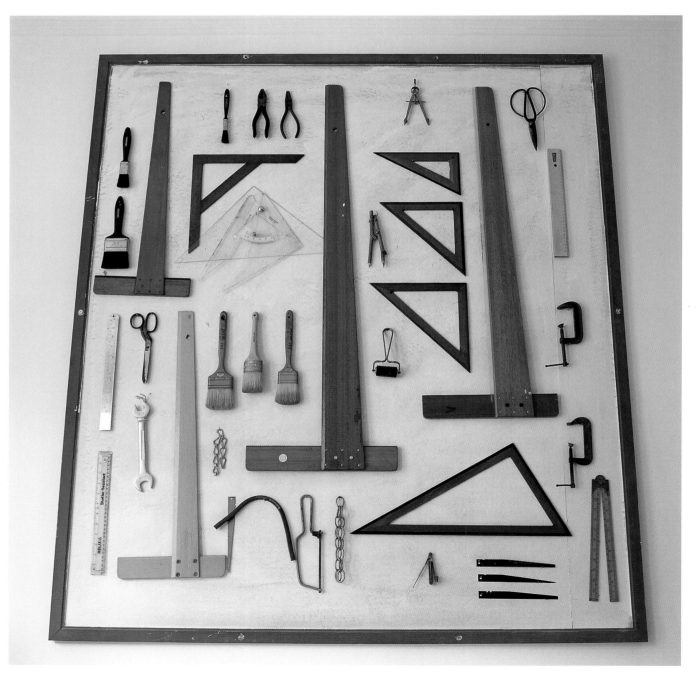

(left) Hugh Henry incorporates a humorous allusion to his profession with this assortment of carpentry and decorating tools and measuring instruments which have been mounted and framed to form a clever and practical wall decoration.

(right) A mahogany folio chest forms a stand for a pair of stoneware vases, a ram's skull and an African mask. A pair of angle poise lights on either side allows the arrangement to be dramatically lit in the evenings.

(opposite) *Every detail in Sir Elton John's bedroom has been carefully chosen to create an ambience that is modern yet sensuous. Candles, fresh flowers in a vase and dried rosebuds in a tazza imbue the air with their delicious scent; a simple column lamp throws a mellow golden light. The bold animal print design of the bed cover is echoed in a marquetry box beside the bed.*

(below) *On the other side of the room an arrangement of art glass brings vivid splashes of colour and light to the muted scheme.*

(right) Sunlight streams in through elegantly draped curtains which are given definition by their dark-fringed edging and dark tie backs. Dark hues are also picked up by a pair of vases on a shelf and an oil painting above. In contrast, the pale sycamore floor matches the wood used for the furniture. Many of the decorative details are inspired by classical design. The pedestal table has a sturdy fluted columnar base; the plinth is inlaid with contrasting burr ash and walnut to complement the tapering legs of the chairs.

(left) Side tables are also accented with geometric designs formed from dark-grained inlays.

(opposite) The feeling of airy spaciousness in Ann Boyd's bedroom is enhanced by filling cupboard door frames with mirror glass. Against one wall a side table provides a surface on which a carefully chosen assortment of objects are grouped. Tall lamps flank a heavy wood-framed mirror. Wooden boxes and a basket container provide useful storage for small items, while beneath more visual interest is provided by a row of prints and photographs propped against the skirting.

(right) The smallest details add to the ambience. Dried lavender and scented candles make the room smell delicious, while (far right) a clever juxtaposition of circular forms provides an unusual visual pun: three balls nestle between a painting of an apple and a bulbous-shaped spherical lamp patterned with interlocking circles.

(below) A glass-topped trestle table in Ann Boyd's bedroom is arranged to reflect her taste for uncluttered simplicity. The large mirror in a limed oak frame increases the light airiness of the room. The curving forms of three stoneware vases set in front subtly tone down the harsh vertical and horizontal lines of mirror and table. Beneath, a pair of storage boxes provide a heavier accent as well as somewhere to hide things away.

(opposite) Our bedroom in the Battersea apartment was designed to combine sensuous luxury with a feeling of spaciousness. The focal point of the room was an antique tester bed, traditionally upholstered with a warm cream and terracotta tapestry. An Aubusson carpet echoed the warm tones; the box on the bedside table was made from ebony and bone, while a silver vase filled with flowers beside it introduced a note of freshness.

(right) The bedroom in our apartment in Battersea. A large marble fireplace was installed to create a warm, welcoming feel as well as to punctuate the wall between the windows. A collection of silver-mounted coconut shells I inherited were set out on the mantelpiece between storm lanterns; a nineteenth-century French clock stood in the centre. The charcoal drawing of camellias above formed a floral link with the upholstery of the armchair and the Aubusson carpet .

(below) A slab of Irish marble quarried at Connemara near where Serena was born embellished an Irish mahogany side table. The silver-framed Victorian mirror was inherited by Serena; the photograph was taken on our engagement. The picture above was by Oliver Messel.

(right) The imaginative design of this guest bedroom designed by Anouska Hempel pushes the boundaries of interior design to new heights. The black and white theme has been applied to every available surface, and every detail is carefully considered. The furniture, supplied by Linley, is made from ebonised wood; the tester beds have elegantly fluted columns that are mirrored in a pair of tall candlesticks standing on the cabinet between them.

(far right) Detail of the master bedroom, another tour de force of theatrical design. The seventeenth-century ebony cabinet provides a stunning foil for a richly upholstered crimson armchair, while tightly clustered roses in a silver trumpet vase provide an exquisite finishing touch.

(left) The dressing room leading from the master bedroom is redolent of gentlemen's clubs. Walls are lined with cupboards made from ebony and mahogany inset with mirrored panels. Polished mahogany floorboards are inset with black slate to match. Lighting is supplied by adjustable lamps attached to brass poles.

(below) Six seventeenth-century silver-framed mirrors grouped together to form a stylish decorative feature in the bedroom.

(right) Bill Blass's bedroom. The surprisingly simple bed is upholstered in a warm paisley fabric and set into a panelled recess. A group of watercolours is carefully arranged above, while Billy Baldwin lamps fitted to the side of the recess ensure there is plenty of light to read by. A window seat covered in ostrich leather stands at the foot of the bed. The dark wood floor is highly polished and adds a note of richness to the simple arrangement, while a large nineteenth-century equestrian bronze of the young Napoleon brings a touch of drama.

(left and above) A classical figure and a mask are among the carefully chosen objects displayed elsewhere in the room.

(below left) Detail of the beautifully crafted paw feet on a pedestal table.

Chapter 7

Working and Playing

THE MODERN TREND TOWARDS MORE FLEXIBLE WORKING HOURS HAS LED INCREASING NUMBERS OF PEOPLE TO DEVOTE PART OF THEIR HOME TO WORK OR SPECIALIST HOBBIES. I PERSONALLY HAVE NEVER WORKED FROM HOME, BUT THE NOTION OF A ROOM ALLOCATED SOLELY FOR WORK IS IMMENSELY APPEALING. ALTHOUGH THERE IS SOME OVERLAP HERE WITH ROOMS DEVOTED TO READING AND WRITING, ROOMS IN WHICH TO WORK RAISE RATHER DIFFERENT CHALLENGES. SHAPED LARGELY BY THE PURSUITS FOR WHICH THEY WILL BE USED, THE POSSIBILITIES OF SUCH ROOMS ARE ENDLESS AND DEFY GEN-ERALISATION. A WORK ROOM'S APPEARANCE DEPENDS ABOVE ALL ON WHAT YOU DO IN IT.

(opposite) Pure white shelving in Alan Fletcher's studio provides an effective backdrop for a humorous assortment of vividly coloured objects. On the top, packaging that appeals to his artistic eye jostles for space with sculpture, an old print and a plastic toy; below, an artist's easel is juxtaposed with a humorous postcard, a stone tortoise, a street number and several boxes; beneath, the quirky decorations include paintbrushes, racing cars, figurines and a set of spectacles.

Similar rules apply to rooms devoted entirely to play: from the ideal nursery, cluttered with bricks and bears, to artists' studios brimming with canvases and brushes, from games rooms to a wine connoisseur's cellar, the rooms that feature on the following pages reveal how ingeniously areas both small and large can be tailored to all manner of pursuits.

The success of a work room depends more on practicality than appearance. For instance, in a studio designed for an artist, sculptor or photographer, aesthetic pleasure comes largely from what is made in the room rather than what the room itself looks like. Nevertheless, as the pictures in this chapter testify, this doesn't mean that artists' studios cannot be visually exciting. One of the most stimulating yet 'undecorated' of work rooms I know is the studio created by Greg Powlesland in his Cornish home. This is a room entirely devoid of self-consciousness, in which Greg paints and sculpts from wood and stone. A sail cloth awning suspended from the ceiling makes you feel as if you're on a boat or in a large tent, although in fact it's there to stop the rain coming in! Clear northern light is of course essential for artists, and the room is surrounded on two sides by windows and set up with a row of spotlights for evening work. A long work bench on one wall is invariably strewn with an amazing amount of creative clutter and tools, while in a corner a pine cupboard made by Greg is filled with assorted woodmaking tools arranged according to size and type, in much the same way as a traditional cabinetmaker would have organised his work chest.

Another work room that is endearing in its muddle is featured on p192. The room is situated in the outhouse of a charming dower house on a large country estate. The owner, an elderly lady, enjoys photography and gardening and has duly made space here for both preoccupations, creating a comfortable room with everything at her fingertips. A work bench provides a useful surface for a light box at one end and a tool box and gardening trug at the other. An old butler's sink and a sunny window sill is useful for propagation of tender plants. A wall plastered with favourite photographs, postcards and watercolours reminds me of my own study at school, which I embellished in a similar manner.

(both pages) I remember watching Greg Powlesland make this cupboard as a store for tools while we were at college. It is arranged in much the same way as eighteenth-century cabinetmakers fitted out chests with groups of chisels and planes.

In the New York apartment belonging to a Swedish financier, interior designer Anouska Hempel created a tiny office that, in contrast to the rest of the apartment (see pp53, 102, 128, 140, 155 and 176–179), is almost completely devoid of distracting decorative elements. The room is furnished only with an elegant walnut-veneered desk and a leather chair set under a large shuttered window. The warm tones of wood and leather are complemented by polished plaster walls, while ebonised panels on the shutters, a sculpture on an ebony plinth and the black-painted skirting board provide subtle accents of contrast.

In our Battersea flat my wife Serena arranged a room in which she could sculpt and paint. Like most studios we kept the decor simple and practical. The north-facing room had large sash windows which we fitted with blinds in order to reduce or vary the light as necessary. Even on the hottest days the room remained pleasantly cool. I recall returning home in the height of summer, boiling hot, to find her working in this lovely room, oblivious to the heat outside. The walls were painted white, and much of the visual interest in the room came from the floor. Originally, this was covered with lino, and when we ripped it up it left the wood underneath roughened, as if it had been sand-blasted. We rather enjoyed the effect and so left it unvarnished.

The furniture in the room was also chosen for its practicality. A store for canvases served as a mobile surface for a TV. The idea was that when children came to sit for her she could turn it on and hopefully they would sit still. There were several wooden boxes which served as seats or platforms of varying heights, also for sitters. Along one wall stood a large pine dresser which provided useful storage for artists' equipment and other assorted treasures: bags of ochre from France were interspersed with family photos, an ostrich egg we collected on our honeymoon, pots of pencils and a well-worn easel.

The library in Stephen Bayley's London home is also organised as somewhere in which his wife Flo, a graphic artist (famously responsible for the design of some of Delia Smith's recent cookery books), can work. The room is situated off the living room, but not where you imagine at first glance. Niches on either side of the fireplace which look as though they're filled with books with a table in front, are in fact filled with nothing but mirrored glass. The work area is opposite. The mirror not only makes the room seem more spacious, it also helps to magnify the light in the room. A galvanised zinc table set in front of a bookcase provides a sizeable

(opposite) A tiny space in a New York apartment designed by Anouska Hempel. The room has been transformed into an uncluttered work room, containing little more than a desk and a chair. The walls have been polished to a bronzed glossy finish that fits well with a burr wood Art Deco writing table and a brown leather chair. An Art Deco lamp with a glass shade stands alongside a stone bust and a plain box. Behind, stained wooden plantation shutters have been given definition to match the black skirting and cornicing with ebonised panels.

work surface, although I can't help feeling it must be chilly on the arms.

The studio created by the graphic designer Alan Fletcher is to my mind the ultimate in witty, modern chic. The walls, floor and furniture are almost entirely white, although there are a couple of black chairs. This blank stage provides Alan with ample room to lay out the book on which he is working on the walls. Yet the room is more than just a serious work place – it is also full of fun. On the desk, in between pots of pens, in trays and so on, is a sculpture made from pencils, and a wig stand on which hats are heaped. On shelves at the far end a variety of toys and other brightly coloured objects are displayed. In front is a mobile made from plastic cutlery, while on the wall is a mosaic made from coloured pencils.

(opposite) A narrow shelf in a bedroom belonging to Stephen Bayley's son, Bruno, provides an adaptable surface on which to paint or construct models. The work surface is supported on industrial-style metal poles and matches the shelving on the adjacent wall.

A wine merchant friend of mine has made an unusual space for what is both work and play to him. Under his dining room floor he has excavated a large area to create an easily accessible wine cellar. A trap door beneath the dining table opens to reveal a spiral staircase descending to a crescent-shaped wine store. The only trouble with this idea is that if the wine runs out during a good dinner, he is often fatally tempted to shift the table and grab a prime bottle or two from the top shelf – and then repent at leisure in the morning when he surveys the empties and realises what has been consumed.

Children's bedrooms provide one of the most demanding of challenges for any parent who wishes to reconcile tidiness with the need to accumulate extensive quantities of books, toys, CDs, or whatever the preoccupation of the moment might be. Stephen Bayley has found a clever answer to these problems in his son Bruno's bedroom. The room is refreshingly free of computers, but there is plenty of space for creative and other interests to develop. One wall is entirely filled with industrial-style open shelving made from planks of polished wood on a metal tube framework. This provides ample space for books, videos, a collection of model motorbikes, racing cars, helicopters and much more besides. Beneath the window a single plank on the same system of metal supports provides a spacious surface on which to make models.

Of course, children don't have a monopoly on play rooms. In Princess Salimah Aga Khan's London home a room has been set aside for card-playing. Plain leather upholstered chairs are arranged around a handsome circular mahogany card table. The table is permanently ready for play, with cards arranged on the baize around a vase of flowers.

There is a similarly well-equipped games room in a large house in upstate New York designed by Greg Jordan. The room has been furnished with a mix of old and new: upholstered chairs make long evenings over hands of bridge a comfortable experience. The card table was made by Linley in 1983, and when not in use provides a stand for a model of the house, also made by us, in which the playing cards are stored. Elegantly swagged curtains in bold red and white stripes lend an air of elegance, while a delightful trompe l'oeil painting of an ace of hearts and flower echoes the card-laying theme. The overall result is a highly sophisticated interior, and one that is full of charm and personality ❖

HAEC DOM

(left) A Linley architectural model of a house is not merely ornamental – it doubles as somewhere to keep cards.
(below far left) Detail of the star-burst design that decorates the top of the table when it is not in play. The opposite side of the reversible top is lined with green baize.
(below left) The date on which the table was made is carved in Latin in the frieze.
(opposite) The table is sturdily built from oak, with bandings of contrasting timber. The legs are tapered and fluted to give a feeling of lightness. The star-burst in each corner echoes the central motif in the top. Four comfortably padded nineteenth-century chairs ensure that you remain seated in comfort however long the evening lasts. As a final finishing touch, the backs are upholstered in a checked fabric that contrasts with the plain fronts.

(left) The work room of this keen photographer and gardener overflows with evidence of her hobbies. The walls are crammed with pictures of flowers, while a light box is set out on a work table, jammed among gardening paraphernalia.

(right) A secret trap door beneath the dining table opens to reveal the hidden cellar of a vintner friend of mine. Bottles are stored in concrete cell-like compartments arranged in a semi-circle.

(both pages) The work room belonging to Flo Bayley is not where you think it is. What seems at first to be an opening is in fact a shallow alcove lined with a mirror: the metal-topped table and well-stocked bookcase behind is on the opposite side of the room.

(both pages) Large quantities of easily accessible storage space are an essential requirement for children's bedrooms. Here, Stephen Bayley has found an effective solution to the problem. An entire wall is filled with open wall-to-ceiling shelving providing ample space for videos, books, toys, models and sporting equipment. The shelving is simply constructed from planks of wood and metal poles, and one section continues under the window to form a work surface.

(left) Details from Greg Powlesland's studio: an assortment of rasps ranged on the work top; work in progress when I last visited was this beautifully carved stone bust of his son, Rupert. (opposite) Traditional homeliness characterises Rupert's nursery. Pine panelling and a door have been used to form a child's cot on which friendly old teddies and other well-loved toys are scattered.

(left) An eighteenth-century circular
card table is permanently set for play
in Princess Salimah Aga Khan's
London home. Elegant leather
upholstered chairs complete the scene
and give a note of masculinity
countered by the simple arrangement of
flowers.

(below) Areas arranged for work and
play in our apartment in Battersea.
A comfortable sofa provided a stand for
my guitar.

(both pages) Serena's studio. Like most
work rooms it was arranged with
practicality in mind. The walls were
painted plain white. An arcaded pine
dresser set against one wall provided
storage for artists' paraphernalia and
personal mementos. In the centre of the
room stood an easel and a tripod stand
for sculpting, and various chairs used
by Serena's sitters. The uneven
parquetry floor remained from when
the building was a school and gave the
room a friendly feel.

(both pages) Designer Alan Fletcher's studio, in which white walls and white utilitarian furniture are livened up by splashes of primary colour and one wall serves as a pin board on which to set out projects. Alan's ingenious sense of fun is evident throughout. On the desk, a sculpture made from a profusion of coloured pencils stands beside a wig stand piled with assorted hats.

Bathrooms rank high among the rooms to have most profited from modern technology. Anyone who harbours a nostalgic longing for life in a previous century only has to ponder what keeping themselves clean would have been like to think again. Few of us would willingly forgo modern washing facilities, however appealing other aspects of day-to-day living in years past may seem.

(opposite) Large mirrors in Ann Boyd's small bathroom maximise the feeling of light and space. Silver accessories and glass shelving give a note of elegant sophistication to make you feel as spotless as your surroundings.

In the twenty-first century household, indoor bathrooms, modern plumbing and hot running water no longer rate as luxuries, but to many of our ancestors they certainly would have been.

Bearing in mind how rapidly architecture advanced over the past half-millennium, it seems strange that plumbing made so few advances from the Middle Ages until the early nineteenth century. Throughout this period indoor bathrooms with running water remained by and large the province of grander houses, although much depended on the location of the buildings, and on the importance their inhabitants attached to keeping clean. The Palace of Westminster had running water in the twelfth century, and by the mid-fourteenth century a bath with hot and cold water was installed. At Windsor Castle, however, which was situated inconveniently (from the point of view of plumbing if not strategically) on top of a hill, running water was not available until a hundred years later. Meanwhile, a variety of ingenious methods were used to bring water to houses. Along with hand pumps and steam pumps (known as engines), treadmills powered by donkeys, horses, and even humans, were all variously used to raise water.

The difficulties of installing running water also hampered the disposal of sewage. Modern lavatories – another installation we all take for granted – have a varied history. Indoor garde robes or jakes (common terms for lavatories in the Middle Ages) were often installed in the upper floors in a special tower or turret set out from the main building. They usually consisted of little more than a seat over a hole connected to a vertical shaft leading to a drain, which often led into the moat. Water closets equipped with their own supply of water to wash out the bowl were developed as early as the sixteenth century, but until the advent of valve closets in the late eighteenth century they were regarded as oddities. Horace Walpole visited a house installed with several water closets and wrote with open-mouthed astonishment of 'conveniences in every bed chamber: great mahogany projections . . . I could not help saying it was the loosest family I ever saw.'

A far more popular alternative to the water closet was the close stool – a portable seat with a chamber pot concealed beneath. In large houses close stools were often decorated as sumptuously as thrones. The King's closet at Knole is furnished with a close stool, on which every available surface, including the seat, is padded and upholstered with red velvet and trimmed with silk braid.

Even though I confess never to have coveted a velvet close stool, I have always felt that bathrooms should be more than merely utilitarian; that as well as being a room in which you can clean yourself effectively, they should be as sensual and pleasurable as possible. In bathrooms, the modern trend for uncluttered simplicity easily tips over into characterless uniformity. But by including something unusual, whether a large item of furniture like a cupboard or a chair, or smaller details such as a bowl of soaps or sponges, bathrooms can easily be instilled with as much personality as any other room.

In our Battersea apartment we combined modern simplicity with a few decorative elements. The bathroom was relatively large, with plain white walls and high ceilings that lent an air of calm to the room. To give warmth to what otherwise might have been

a rather cold, impersonal room, we used curl-figured mahogany panelling for cupboard doors and to surround the bath. The mirrors over the basins were in fact cupboards, which helped to alleviate the inevitable clutter. The taps were of nickel, which has a particularly lustrous finish. Among the more unusual items we included were a pair of eighteenth-century chairs that I inherited from Oliver Messel's house, Maddox, in Barbados, and restored to their former glory. These looked good and were useful for depositing clothes and towels. Elsewhere, an old 1930s planter's chair provided somewhere to relax, and a painted French cupboard from Judy Greenwood was useful for storing linen, sponges and brushes as well as soaps that helped make the room smell delicious. On the walls we hung a few paintings that held personal associations by Serena, Sarah Armstrong Jones, and various friends of ours.

Even the smallest of bathrooms can be imaginatively transformed into somewhere that is both pleasurable and sensuous with a few clever touches. With its tiled floor, old-fashioned bath and pedestal hand basin, the modestly proportioned bathroom in Hugh Henry's flat has an air of traditional homeliness, yet several clever touches set it apart. The walls are adorned with a series of prints of human anatomy, and a frame of identical size has been used for a mirror above the hand basin. The anatomical theme

(both pages) Hugh Henry imbues his bathroom with some ingenious finishing touches.
(left) The shelves of a painted armoire are fitted with wicker baskets that neatly hide clutter, and the door is fronted with a lattice of cord.
(right) A table made from animal bone forms an unusual bath-side stand on which to display a pot of dried leaves. A traditional chrome bath rack slung over the bath provides space to store some attractive bathroom accessories.

continues with a small side table, the pedestal of which is constructed from elephant bones. A tiny shower room in the same apartment is also imaginatively adorned with Russian propaganda porcelain plates that have been arranged in sets of four in bright red frames that complement the geometric patterns of the porcelain.

In the bathroom designed by John McCall, modern, high-quality bathroom fittings are similarly combined with the odd quirky touch. The walls, ceiling, bath and cupboard doors are beautifully panelled with generous stepped mouldings that add an air of opulence to the room. The shower is brightly lit and has a nice large rose to provide an ample supply of water. The lavatory is ingeniously fitted inside an eighteenth-century-style close stool in the form of an armchair, so that when not in use it looks to all intents and purposes like a rather sophisticated painted chair.

Ann Boyd has used the traditional trinity of white, glass and silver in her small bathroom to create a pristine effect. A traditional chrome towel rail is reflected elsewhere in silver tooth mug and jars. The walls, towels and sanitaryware are all white, while the shelving is made from glass. I imagine it would be impossible to come out of here and not feel as immaculate as the surroundings you'd just left.

In the sumptuous New York apartment designed by Anouska Hempel for a Swedish financier, black slate and white marble are used to create a highly theatrical master bathroom that continues the bold black and white theme of the bedroom and dressing room (see pp155 and 178). The bathroom is entered through double doors leading from the dressing room. In front is the bath, positioned end on, on a raised platform of black slate and white marble. On the left is the door to the shower and on the right the hand basin. The same materials have been used throughout in contrasting geometric patterns, on the floor, to line the bath, and facing the shower. Although the bathroom is not large, what strikes you most is the way in which everything has been finished to the highest level of excellence. Look at the way the slate corners have been cut in soft curves, the way the edge of every mirror has been bevelled; the mirrors even have heated pads behind them so they never steam up when the bathroom is in use.

Elsewhere in the same apartment are two similarly imaginative cloakrooms. The first, off the entrance hall, features a slender crescent-shaped wash basin carved from solid slate in the manner of an eighteenth-century buffet. The lovely matte sheen of the stone is complemented by a mirror in a simple ridged black frame and by gleaming yellow walls specially finished by Sheila Sartin. Another cloakroom is decorated with

Japanese-style austerity. Against black walls a shallow, circular white ceramic basin is set into simple oak decking with plain chrome taps suspended over it and set into the floor-length mirror behind.

Finally, one of the most originally positioned water features I discovered during my research for this chapter was planted in Stephen Bayley's house. Originally made for a ship, this chrome water fountain folded up flush to the wall when not in use, and unfolded rather like a drop-leaf desk when you wanted it. Anyone suddenly overcome by thirst or the thought that their hands need rinsing while walking past has nothing to fear. I wonder how often it is used ❖

(left) A chrome water fountain salvaged from an old ship forms an unusual feature in Stephen Bayley's house. (opposite) Clean lines and pleasing textures are emphasised in this wash room designed by Anouska Hempel. A black wall provides a dramatic foil for a shallow white porcelain bowl placed on a slatted stand. Simple taps are set into a mirror behind.

(left) Imposing grandeur is evoked by this bathroom design by Anouska Hempel. Panels of black slate and white marble, interspersed with large mirrors, form a recurring theme. The design is a striking one: the bath is at the far end of the room and set on a higher level than the basin and shower. (right) A cloakroom in the same apartment is treated with similar imaginative flair. The wash basin is cut from polished black slate in a shallow elliptical form. A simple gadroon-framed mirror reflects a sketch by Tim Gosling in an identical mount; a tall candlestick adds height to the arrangement.

(both pages) The bathroom in our Battersea apartment. Ample space and height allowed us to create a room that was both practical and sensual. Sponges and bath oils were lined up along the edge of the panelled bath. The basins behind were set into a marble top; a pair of mahogany-framed mirrors above concealed shallow cupboards. On the opposite wall a softly painted French armoire offered space to store towels. Hanging on it is a beautifully embroidered Equadorian bolero. The pictures include a sketch by Tony Fry, a chalk study by Serena and a Picasso lithograph.

(both pages) Convention is given an unusual twist in this handsome bathroom designed by John McCall. The lavatory is fitted into a hinged armchair, while panelling shrouds walls, bath and cupboard doors, and is painted a soft shade of green. Restrained colour highlights textures and finishes. The shower is operated by a pair of traditional porcelain and chrome handles set into a marble surround. The shower rose is a traditional design guaranteed to supply a generous drenching. Green-tinged glass shelves set between the shower and basin create an attractive space on which to display bottles.

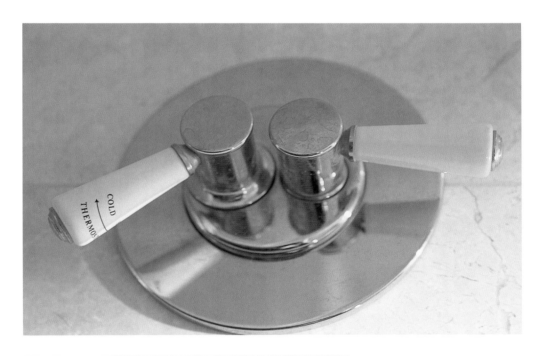

Bibliography & Acknowledgements

Girouard, M., *Life in the English Country House*, Yale University Press, 1994

Hardyment, C., *Behind the Scenes – Domestic Arrangements in Historic Houses*, The National Trust, 1997

Hibbert, C., *The English, A Social History 1066–1945*, HarperCollins, 1988

Jackson-Stops, G. and Pipkin, J., *The English Country House: A Grand Tour*, Seven Dials, 1998

Gloag, J., *Georgian Grace*, 1956

Latham , R. (ed), *The Shorter Pepys*, University of California Press, 1985

Payne, C. (ed), *Sotheby's Concise Encyclopaedia of Furniture*, Bounty Books, 1998

Pottle, F. A. (ed), *Boswell's London Journal*, Edinburgh University Press, 1991

Richardson, A. E., *Georgian England*, Ayer Co., 1931

ACKNOWLEDGEMENTS

The author would like to thank the following individuals and institutions for their generous help: Charles Allen, Alidad, Stephen Bayley, Bill Blass, Derek Boon, Ann Boyd, Andrew Bruce, Nina Campbell, Charles Cator, Peter Dixon, Valerie Finnis, Alan Fletcher, Viscount Folkestone, Anthony and Juliet Hardman, Oliver Heal, Anouska Hempel Designs, Hugh Henry, Kelly Hoppen, Sir Elton John, Greg Jordan, Princess Salimah Aga Khan, Walter Lees, Alain and Caroline Levy, Eddie and Miranda Lim, Christopher Little, John McCall, Yvonne Miller, Tara and Sasha O'Keefe, Greg and Lavinia Powlesland, The Earl and Countess of Radnor, Fritz von der Schulenburg, The Earl of Snowdon, Catherine Soames, Michael and Lorraine Spencer, John and Sarah Standing, Jane Taylor, Phillip Wagner, Steve de Wet, Stephen White, Sarah Wright.

David Linley & Company Limited

60 Pimlico Road

London SW1 W8LP

Telephone +44 (020) 7730 7300

Facsimile +44 (020) 7730 8869

E-mail linley@davidlinley.com

Website www.davidlinley.com